P9-BBV-914

THEY CALL ME

SPARKY

BY

Sparky Anderson

WITH

Dan Ewald

Sleeping Bear Press
121 South Main
P.O. Box 20
Chelsea, MI 48118
www.sleepingbearpress.com

Printed and bound in Canada by Friesen's, Altona, Manitoba.

10 9 8 7 6 5 4 3 2 1

Cataloging-in-Publication Data on file.
ISBN 1-886947-23-6
Cover photo courtesy of Alan Lowy Photography.

Acknowledgment

It's impossible to personally thank all the individuals who have given so much to me since my days as a young boy. Without my wife, Carol, and our three children, Lee, Shirlee, and Albert, nothing would have meant a thing. My mother and father will live forever in my heart.

I owe so much to so many people in baseball—from those who have gone on to the Hall of Fame to those who played a reserve role—I thank you so much.

Most of all, to every young boy or girl who has a dream and wishes to live honestly and with integrity, this book is for you.

Sparky Anderson

Contents

Introduction

How much money does it take for a person to be considered a success?

A million dollars? Two million? Ten million?

How about none of the above? How about just a dime and a smile?

Success is one of those sneaky words that can trick an Einstein into looking like a dummy.

It's a sucker term. Sometimes it makes my stomach shiver.

A lot of people think I twist words so much they wind up looking like a pretzel. The writers call them "Sparkyisms."

They're right. I don't always get the right word in the right place at the right time. Sometimes I might even make up a word if it fits better than any of the words I know.

I don't make no mistakes about success, though. That's one word I understand right down to the bone.

I know if you try to judge success by the amount of money a person makes then you don't have a clue about what it really means.

Success don't have nothing to do with how much money somebody makes. Someone can have his pockets stuffed with hundred dollar bills and not be as successful as the guy who has to put all his change together to buy a couple of coney islands.

The rich guy is only more fortunate.

I don't know how we ever fell off the track to think a

man or a woman is better than anyone else just because they make more money. When it comes to people, there ain't nobody in the world better than anybody else.

Just because a doctor might make more money, he's no better than a painter. A lawyer ain't better than a plumber. A banker ain't better than a bus driver. A ball player, manager or any kind of athlete ain't no better than the man or woman sitting up in one of those luxury suites in a new ballpark or the kid who parks their cars for tips.

And nobody's better than anybody else just because of the color of his skin!

I hate that bumper sticker that says "the winner is the guy who winds up with the most toys." Getting all the toys in the world don't mean a lick if you ain't got nobody to play with.

I know that teachers don't make a whole lot of money. Yet every day, they probably touch more young lives than any rich businessman sitting in a fancy office on the top floor of some building that reaches up to the clouds.

A lot of people might say now that I've made a lot of money in my career, it's easy for me to talk like this. I've been blessed. I have made more money than I ever thought possible.

But that don't make me better than anyone else.

Our society comes up with some pretty funny ideas. A lot of people think that if a person is poor, then he must be stupid.

Let me tell you something straight. My daddy wasn't stupid!

He was a painter and raised five kids. He went from paycheck to paycheck and sometimes had to tap into the next month.

And he was one of the wisest men I've ever known.

I'll guarantee you there are more happy people that don't have all kinds of material things who are a whole lot happier than those people living in Beverly Hills and driving all those fancy cars.

I'm writing this book for only one reason. I want all people, and especially the young ones, to realize what the really important things in life are.

I've made a lot of mistakes. I'll share some with you.

Everybody on God's earth makes a bundle of mistakes. Anybody can make an error. If you don't ever fumble the ball, then you ain't never been in the game. That's why we have scorecards and pencils with erasers.

But I never made the one mistake of making money my goal. I never stepped on other people and forgot that everybody else is a human being, too.

I've been so fortunate in baseball, sometimes I still pinch myself to make sure it all ain't a dream. I've managed in five World Series and five All-Star Games. I've met presidents, celebrities and movie stars. I've even met the Pope. He didn't know who in the heck this Sparky character was, but he touched me like no other person has. I'll never forget that peaceful look in his eyes.

But the money and all the good things that happened to me came for only one reason—I was more fortunate. I worked as hard as I could. I followed my dream. But I always stayed true to the principles my daddy taught me and caught a few breaks along the way.

Not once when I started in baseball did I ever set money as my goal. I only wanted to work hard and do the very best job I could. I only wanted to be a credit to baseball and make all of my family and friends proud.

I get a kick out of some parents today. They send their kids to college so they can get a better job and make more money than the old man ever did.

Is that what education is supposed to be all about?

College is a wonderful thing. But what about going to college to learn what life is really about? What about teaching our kids that the real reward in life is not in how many dollars they make, but in how much good they can do for the less fortunate?

When the scorekeeper makes his final count, I don't think he'll be standing there with a cash register. A person has to satisfy himself. And there's no greater satisfaction than being able to help those who need a hand.

There's a lot of money in our society today. More than I could have ever imagined. A lot of that money is in professional sports. Sometimes I think it's Monopoly money because it seems so make-believe.

I think it's marvelous for the athlete to make as much as he can. But don't for one second think a dollar comes without a responsibility to every child in America regardless if you're a player or a doctor or an Indian chief.

Athletes who say they ain't role models for our youth are dumber than Bozo. They don't deserve a dime of their millions. They're totally missing the boat. God gave them all this special ability and then they take the money and snub their noses at the kids or anybody who happens to be in their way.

They've got to understand that they have the chance to be a leader. They can teach our young by the way they live their lives.

Whether they like it or not, every athlete is a role model. So is every adult. Our children look up to us. Every day, we get the chance to influence more young lives than we can ever imagine.

Sometimes it just takes a smile or a little pat on the shoulder. Maybe all it takes is a couple of minutes to listen to a youngster's problem.

I believe if an athlete does something dumb like getting hooked on alcohol or drugs, then he should be penalized double. That's the price for the precious gift they've been given.

All that drugs and alcohol prove is that a person is scared. He's scared to face the reality we all must deal with day after day. He hides behind the bottle or a needle or a pill. I don't want to be around anyone who needs booze or drugs to feel brave.

That guy's a coward. And I ain't seen a coward yet who isn't the biggest loser in the world.

When I managed at Cincinnati, I had a wonderful shortstop from Venezuela by the name of David Concepcion. He was just a young man at the time, but it was easy to see he would quickly become a star.

When David's son, Alejandro, was born, I remember telling David this story.

"David, do yourself and Alejandro a favor. Take him to the poor section of town each day and let him play with those children. He'll wind up being a much better man for it some day."

Don't get me wrong. There's nothing wrong with making money. But let it happen without making it your goal. Strive to do your best. Never allow yourself to give anything less than all you've got. Lend a hand to those who might need a little lift. And then just let things happen.

I ain't no better than anybody else. And neither are you.

We're all blessed with the same gift of opportunity. And there ain't nothing more precious than the chance to help kids to do the right thing.

This book is for the kids. And also for all of us big kids who really have the chance to make a difference.

Sparky Anderson

Statistical Legacy

George Lee "Sparky" Anderson's statistical legacy to baseball serves as the yardstick for all modern major league managers. Only Hall of Famers Connie Mack and John McGraw surpassed his 2,194 in victories in the history of the game.

Sparky, however, notched a few firsts and various other milestones of his own which will go unchallenged for many years.

- He is the only manager to lead two franchises in all-time victories—Cincinnati (863) and Detroit (1,331).
- He is the only manager in history to lead teams to World Series championships in both the American and National Leagues.
- He is the only manager to record a 100-win season in each league.
- He won three World Series (1975, 1976 and 1984).
- He was named Manager of the Year twice in the National League (1972 and 1975) and twice in the American League (1984 and 1987).
- He is one of only four men to have managed at least 4,000 major league games (4,028). The others are Connie Mack (7,679), John McGraw (4,711), and Bucky Harris (4,375).
- He is one of only seven men to have managed at least 25 years in the major leagues. They are: Connie Mack (53), John McGraw (33), Bucky Harris

(29), Sparky Anderson (26), Gene Mauch (26), Bill McKechnie (25), and Casey Stengel (25).

Sparky spent 10 years as a minor league infielder. His best season was 1954 when he batted .296 with no homers and 62 RBI for Pueblo. His one major league season was 1959 with the Philadelphia Phillies. He batted .218 with no homers and 34 RBI in 152 games.

He managed five years in the minor leagues and spent 1969 as a coach for the San Diego Padres before being named manager of the Cincinnati Reds at the age of 35 in October, 1969.

Sparky was born on February 22, 1934 in Bridgewater, SD. His family moved to Los Angeles when he was nine years old. He married Carol Valle in 1953. They live in the same house they built in 1967 in Thousand Oaks, CA. They have three children—Lee, Shirlee, and Albert and 14 grandchildren.

Here is Sparky's lifetime major league managerial record:

YEAR	CLUB	POSITION	W–L
1970	Cincinnati	1	102–60
1971	Cincinnati	T4	79–83
1972	Cincinnati	1	95–59
1973	Cincinnati	1	99–63
1974	Cincinnati	2	98–64
1975	Cincinnati	1	108–54
1976	Cincinnati	1	102–60
1977	Cincinnati	2	88–74
1978	Cincinnati	2	92–69
1979	Detroit	5	56–50
1980	Detroit	5	84–78
1981	Detroit	4	31–26
		T2	29–23
1982	Detroit	4	83–79
1983	Detroit	2	92–70
1984	Detroit	1	104–58

1985	Detroit	3	84–77
1986	Detroit	3	87–75
1987	Detroit	1	98–64
1988	Detroit	2	88–74
1989	Detroit	7	59–103
1990	Detroit	3	79–83
1991	Detroit	2	84–78
1992	Detroit	6	75–87
1993	Detroit	T3	85–77
1994	Detroit	5	53–62
1995	Detroit	4	60–84
TOTALS		26 years	2194–1834

Putting It on the Line

In a couple of years, Sparky Anderson and his entire family will travel cross-country to spend a weekend in Cooperstown, New York.

Although quaint and bursting with old world charm, it's not the most typical choice of a place for a California family to spend a few summer days. Of course, this will be no ordinary vacation.

The whole Anderson family—and who knows how many thousands of other friends and fans from around the country—will convene to celebrate the grandest professional moment of Sparky's colorful career.

That's when Sparky will be inducted into the National Baseball Hall of Fame.

With five World Series, five All-Star Games, three World Championships, including at least one in each league, and more victories than only two managers in history, Sparky's election awaits only his year of eligibility, which is 2000, after he turns sixty-five.

Sparky's niche in the Hall of Fame is as much of a lock as next year's taxes.

"If he doesn't make it on the first ballot there has to be an investigation," said Hall of Fame Manager Tommy Lasorda. "He's done things no other manager in history ever has done. And he's meant so much for the color of the game. If he doesn't make it, there is no Hall of Fame."

Except for only three already enshrined members of the Hall, Sparky managed more games than anyone in history. After 4,028 games covering 26 years as a major league manager, Sparky figured he had encountered every challenge imaginable to a professional sports leader.

Then along came 1995 spring training and baseball created a monster like no one had ever seen before. With it, Sparky was faced with the stiffest personal test of his life.

This one didn't test his baseball expertise. Nothing can question Sparky's baseball savvy and long list of accomplishments. There are whole chapters in baseball's record books that justify his elevated stature in the game's history.

This test was different. It dared him to make a choice. And the ramifications of that choice stretched far beyond the foul lines of any baseball diamond in America.

Sparky was put in a face-to-face showdown of choosing between job security and his lifelong commitment to principle.

This kind of decision rarely comes along in any person's life. There is, in fact, no greater moment of character definition.

In spite of risking his position as manager of the Detroit Tigers . . . in spite of jeopardizing his very future in the game . . . Sparky answered the call. He refused to manage replacement players.

Sparky looked at the replacement situation a little bit differently than the rest of those in baseball. His first concern was integrity. Not just the integrity that had been instilled in him when he was a child, but all the principles he had preached to his players throughout his career.

That meant more than his million dollar-plus salary. If principle is truly pure, no long ribbon of zeroes at the end of a paycheck figure should ever compromise integrity.

It was really pretty simple. Principle can't be measured in dollars and cents.

At least that's the way Sparky believes it's supposed to be. And he had a chance to prove his commitment.

The temptation to compromise was enticing. In the end, no amount of money could have cracked his resolve. When the affair was finally over, he admitted his decision was the "proudest moment of my career."

In 1995 spring training, major league baseball had

reached one of the lowest points in its labor relations history. The situation had gone from ridiculous to absurd. Because of it, in fact, baseball's fracture with many fans has yet to be healed.

Major league players had walked away from the game over negotiations for a new basic agreement with the owners the previous August. In mid-September, the owners incredibly canceled the Playoffs and World Series of 1994.

For most of the century, baseball basked in its role of "America's pastime." For the most part, it had gone relatively unchallenged in its domination of sports. Cancellation of the national tradition was unforgivable.

But what baseball initiated the following spring training bordered on sacrilege, even to borderline fans.

Without settlement with the players association, the owners threatened to open the 1995 season with replacement players for the regular major leaguers.

For the most part, these replacements were not minor league players already under contract to the 28 major league clubs. The majority of the replacements were retired minor leaguers and former college, high school, and sandlot players.

Some of the recruits had not played organized baseball for a number of years. Teams were instructed to assemble the best available talent. Many clubs conducted open tryout camps in their Florida and Arizona spring training bases.

For the entire spring training exhibition season, each club used replacements. These imitation major leaguers were not disbanded until the day before the regular season was scheduled to start. Only then did the owners concede to allowing the real major leaguers back to play while an agreement was negotiated.

Except for Sparky Anderson, no other major league manager refused to manage replacements. The Toronto Blue Jays allowed Cito Gaston and his coaching staff to work with minor leaguers until a settlement was reached. The other 26 major league managers worked with replacements.

Sparky carefully explained that his refusal to manage replacements was not intended to support the striking major league players. He was equally careful not to lend political support to the owners.

For Sparky, this was not a political matter. His decision was based on something much simpler. It was integrity.

He believed the use of make-believe major leaguers threatened the moral conscience of the game.

"Everyone was in a kind of panic stage," said long-time Detroit Tiger shortstop Alan Trammell. "Sparky's a little different. He thought, 'Wait a minute. I've got my principles. This is a joke.' When it gets down to a matter of ethics, Sparky Anderson is not going to be part of any joke. No amount of money and no kind of threat to his job security would ever make Sparky compromise what he believes in."

If the baseball owners had figured Sparky would go along with the masquerade, they were quickly corrected.

"People misread him," said Billy Consolo, former Detroit Tiger coach and friend of Sparky since childhood days. "He wasn't for the players. He wasn't for the owners. He was thinking of baseball. There was a separation and people couldn't make that distinction.

"You have to know him from a kid. It was always baseball and always the right thing to do. If the owners ever read anything about Sparky Anderson, they would have known that principles come first."

Sparky remained silent about his decision throughout the winter after the owners announced their replacement scheme. From the day of its inception, Sparky's mind was determined. All that remained was the execution of his decision.

"Sparky is not a hypocrite," said former Detroit Tiger great Kirk Gibson.

"He constantly preached principles to his players his whole career. For him to manage those replacement players would have been wrong for the game. It went against everything he had ever told anyone who had ever played for him."

Even those outside the game felt the significance of Sparky's decision. Sparky received a flood of mail from everyday people from around the country. Almost all of it was supportive. Even those who weren't diehard baseball fans were moved by Sparky's conviction.

"He knew he had to walk the walk," said Lee Anderson, Sparky's oldest son. "Over the years, my dad always talked to kids about how education and living the right way is more important than making a lot of money. After teaching that his whole life, how could he do nothing and just take the money? He had to stand up for what he believed in. He did the right thing. He made me very proud."

Sparky met recently appointed Tiger President John McHale, Jr. in Orlando, Florida a few nights before the scheduled opening of spring training in nearby Lakeland. McHale did not try to dissuade Sparky's decision. He asked, however, if Sparky would simply go on the field in the minor league camp with the replacements.

Sparky refused to compromise his commitment.

Two nights later, Sparky received a call from Acting Baseball Commissioner Bud Selig who simply asked how Sparky would have handled the strike situation.

"Put locks on all the spring training doors and hide all the keys till the thing is settled," Sparky answered.

Sparky also told Selig that baseball would never open the regular season with replacements. And it didn't.

The day before spring training opened, the Tigers placed Sparky on an unpaid leave of absence.

"Sparky had a hefty chunk of change sitting on the table," said former Tiger catcher Lance Parrish. "That's a pretty strong sacrifice for somebody to make if they don't have to. I think a lot of people gained a whole new level of respect for him when he made that stand.

"It wasn't a slap in the face to the replacement players. It was a disgrace for the game to go through something like that and he wasn't going to be part of it. I always respected Sparky, but I gained a little more for him. I'm sure there were a few managers who thought about doing it, but only Sparky followed through."

The owners, of course, were appalled. Even some of Sparky's closest friends did not totally agree with his decision.

"We can't all agree on that thing," said Rod Dedeaux.

Dedeaux is the former University of Southern California baseball coach who holds the NCAA record of 11 national championships. He also owns one of the most successful trucking companies in the state of California. When Sparky was a boy, he served as one of Dedeaux's batboys.

"Being in business myself, I knew where the owners were coming from," Dedeaux added. "But I totally admired him and the stance he took. It wasn't an emotional decision done on the spur of the moment. He thought it out thoroughly and stuck with it. Whether you agreed with him or not, anybody would have to totally admire him for that position."

On the day he was placed on his unpaid leave, Sparky held a press conference in his stadium office. The crowd it attracted resembled a scene from the World Series. The room was packed with writers from spring training camps from around the state of Florida. The crowd of photographers looked like a herd of paparazzi gathering for a night out with Madonna.

Sparky realized he may have managed his last major league game. By the time he boarded the plane to his daughter's home in Sacramento the next day, stories already had begun to circulate in Florida that the Tiger owner had wanted him fired immediately.

"If he got fired, he got fired," Gibson explained. "Sparky thought about it and said no. He didn't give a damn if he ever managed another game again. They were making a fiasco out of the game and he wasn't going to be part of it. His decision showed how much he loves the game."

Sparky had demonstrated a love and respect for the game ever since he was a boy on the sandlots. It didn't matter at which level he participated. No one person was bigger than the game.

"I remember the first time I sat on the bench and saw him manage the Tigers," Consolo recalled. "Some player struck out and came back to the bench ranting and raving, 'Damn this game of baseball.' Probably every kid who has struck out at some point has said the same thing. But not around Sparky Anderson. You do not belittle the game around him. He jumped on that kid so fast he didn't know what hit him."

Commitment like that transcends the game. It's Sparky's interpretation of everything he believes important in life.

"Sparky loves the game," Consolo said. "That's why he walked out."

The walkout cost Sparky $150,000 of his salary. And once he returned, he didn't get a penny of it back.

The walkout also cost him any chance of returning to the Tigers in 1996. At the time, he was in the final season of a multiyear contract.

"I knew for sure I wouldn't be back with the Tigers the following year," he admitted. "There was no way they wanted me back. And I knew there was no way I would have gone back. Not after some of the things I heard that were said about me."

The moment he announced he would not manage replacement players, speculation exploded over whether Sparky had managed his last game. Even before Sparky left town, unconfirmed reports trickled from Detroit indicating certain segments of ownership wanted him fired immediately.

As his absence continued, that speculation increased. Members of the Detroit media on assignment to spring training in Florida adjusted their daily odds on whether Sparky would ever return.

It was widely speculated that McHale had to convince ownership to keep Sparky through the end of his contract.

McHale prevailed and Sparky returned for the abbreviated 1995 season.

"I understand why Sparky did what he did," said all-time hits leader Pete Rose, who played nine years for Sparky at Cincinnati. "Most other guys wouldn't have done it because they'd be scared they'd be fired. Sparky was big on principles. He didn't do it as a crusader. He did it for peace with himself. I wasn't surprised."

Baseball and the major league players association didn't reach a formal agreement until well into the 1996 season. By that time, Sparky was getting used to spending his first season out of the game after 43 years in professional baseball.

"If he had to do it over again, he'd do the same thing," Gibson said. "You hate to see what's happening in the game today. The game is still a game—a real game. You have a hard time finding out what the real game of baseball is today. Sparky has strong feelings about the game of baseball and the professionalism that belongs in it. Sparky's made his share of mistakes, but never one that would embarrass the game."

The decision of 1995 became Sparky's proudest moment. It won't appear on his plaque in Cooperstown. But it will be valued by true baseball fans—as well as anyone who appreciates commitment to principle—as much as any of those 2,194 wins.

Anyone who places principle above fear of repercussion still shares in Sparky's defining moment.

"He didn't let money or the threat of never managing again change what he believed in," said Sparky's daughter, Shirlee. "How many people do that? He was true to himself.

"Other than my children, I don't love anything with a passion like that. To think he loved baseball so much is pretty incredible."

Sparky's "proudest moment" belongs not only to the man who made the decision of his lifetime, but also to anyone who places principles above all monetary considerations.

The Right Thing . . . The Only Thing

I ain't no martyr. I ain't no hero. And I don't want no bowl of chocolate ice cream, whipped cream and cherries just for doing the right thing.

My daddy never raised me to be a hero. But he damn sure taught me always to do the right thing, no matter what it cost.

I know I did the right thing in 1995. Now, when I look back at everything that happened then, I got to believe I was the luckiest man in the world.

How many people get the chance to stand up for everything they've believed in ever since they were a kid? For me it was baseball. Not just the game itself, but all the good it's stood for ever since the first pitch was thrown.

At some point in everybody's life, you just got to look that monster in the eye. You dare him to bite, and worry about what might happen later.

I got that chance. And I'd be lying if I told you that my stomach wasn't doing flips when I thought about all the things that could happen if I decided that I wouldn't manage the replacement players.

I knew I was going to lose a bundle of money. That was the easy part. I also knew there was the very real possibility that I might never manage again.

More than anything else, I knew the right thing to do. There was no other choice. Until I finally told them, though, I wasn't sure if I had the guts.

When I left spring training in Florida and got on that plane for Sacramento, I finally realized I had passed the test. Right at that moment, I knew I had accomplished everything I ever wanted to accomplish in my lifetime.

Strange, but it was the proudest moment of my career.

A lot of this stuff had been building up in me for a long time. It seemed like for the last ten years, every time we turned around there was another player strike. Clubs started coming up with so many marketing gimmicks, I thought one day I'd show up to the park and my uniform would have a big advertisement sewed on the back.

We kept creeping away from what the game is really about. It seems like we forgot that baseball is supposed to be fun and belongs to the kids and families all over the world.

When the baseball owners canceled the World Series in 1994, I was almost paralyzed. It was like getting hit below the belt with a bowling ball. I knew right then and there that this isn't the game that I came into . . . this isn't the game that I knew . . . and this certainly isn't the game that I loved totally with all my heart.

Then as that winter went on and I started to hear about replacement players, I thought I had to get my ears checked. I thought I must have fallen into *The Twilight Zone.*

I couldn't believe that grown men who are supposed to have common sense could actually come up with the idea of using replacement players. They were actually going to bring in some guys who never played in eight to ten years and call it major league baseball!

What if a teachers' union went on strike? Would the school board drive around the city to hire a bunch of people who weren't busy, just to keep the classes open?

What about the history of the game? What about integrity? What about how much it means to the kids and all the fans who ever followed the game?

What kind of message were we telling little Johnny? 'Don't worry if you run into a problem in life, Johnny. We'll just change the rules and everything will be all right.'

This was truly laughable. People were going to laugh at us. Worse than that, they were putting a price tag on everything we are supposed to hold sacred.

I remember watching a baseball special on TV that showed all the players who starred in the old Negro Leagues. They were never allowed to play in the majors just because they were black. How could we have ever been so stupid? It was like a nightmare.

Now along comes this replacement thing and we're ready to make another nightmare all over again. We were willing to sacrifice our history and everything we believed in, all on account of money!

Well, not me!

Some day down the line, I figured someone is going to film a documentary on this replacement fiasco. I promised myself right then and there that my name would never be attached to it.

When they run that thing on TV, my grandkids won't see Grandpa's face on it unless they say—here's the only guy who didn't show up at Mardi Gras. Maybe they can put a picture of me in there and say that "he's the one that stood up and refused to go."

I'm grateful for all the wonderful things that baseball has done for me and my family. How could I betray all of that by taking part in this replacement thing?

My whole life I taught all my kids and all my players the same lesson. You're a human being. When you're born, you automatically come into this world with class. Now you can do one of two things. You can keep it . . . or you can give it away.

There ain't no price tag on class. You can't measure

class in dollars and cents. You might not have no money. But if you keep your class, you're richer than all those wealthy people who got their money by selling off their class.

I'd rather have class than money. When I go to the grave, the money won't do me no good. I ain't gonna go floating up in the clouds sitting in a Mercedes Benz . . . even though I actually drive a Probe.

If I keep my class, that's the way people will remember me. They'll always say—'the man had class.'

How could I have managed those replacement players and ever looked any of my real players in the eye? Not after preaching about class to them my whole career.

To this day, I ain't sure everybody understood exactly why I did what I had to do.

I didn't refuse to manage so that I could side with the players. I never took a side with the owners, either. And for damn sure I never felt nothing against the replacement players themselves. They were being used. They were just ploys. I had more compassion for them than anyone realized.

I usually like to joke around with the media. I've done it my whole career. But I wasn't joking that day when I held a press conference to tell them I was going home. I got more serious than a priest giving the last rites.

I tried to tell them I wasn't taking sides with the players or owners. What I was doing was strictly for baseball. Using replacement players was wrong. It didn't help the game. It embarrassed it.

There was no way I could ever do anything that would embarrass the game of baseball. And if just one person learned about the importance of standing up for what he believes in, then it was all worth it.

The press conference gave me an eerie feeling. I kept thinking this might be the last one I'm ever asked to do.

All winter long, my wife, Carol, and I talked about what might happen to me. And, believe me, she stood right behind me one hundred percent. Carol knows the right thing to do. She's stronger than me. Ain't nothing gonna intimidate her.

We knew there was a chance I might be fired on the spot. There was a lot of money at stake. Carol reminded me I never got into the game to make a lot of money. If it cost me every penny I had, they were welcome to it. There ain't enough money around to make me give in when I know I'm doing the right thing.

By the time I left Florida, I already heard the rumors about the owner wanting me fired. I believe he did. And, in all fairness, I can understand his position. He had a ball club and his guy walked. There were 27 other managers and I didn't see no parade following me down the highway.

But I really didn't want no entourage. There were a lot of young managers and I didn't want their blood on my hands. I think a lot of them felt that if they followed me, they might not ever manage again. Everyone had to make their own decision.

My only disappointment came from a few of the boys who spoke out against what I did. I won't mention names. They know who they are. Everyone has a right to his opinion. But if you're gonna talk the talk, then put your wallet on the table before you open your mouth. If you got the guts to risk over one million dollars, I want to hear what you have to say. All the money on the table was mine. Nobody matched the ante.

When I left, I thought the odds were against me coming back. I'll tell you the truth—and swear under oath—I really didn't care. I knew I was right.

If I had never been asked back, it probably would have hurt more than I could imagine. But I'll swear under oath again, I never regretted my decision for a second.

I never cried over a penny that my leave of absence cost me. I'd do the same thing a thousand times over. The next time, though, I'd do it even quicker.

My decision was a bombshell. If the owners thought I betrayed them, they missed the whole point. That wasn't the case at all. The only thing I wouldn't do was betray baseball. I wasn't going to try to fool the fans who pay for the games.

And no way under the sun was I gonna betray the principles my daddy taught me.

The money has gotten too big. Ain't it a shame that we seem to judge everything today on the amount of money we can make?

Doesn't it mean something for a baseball player just to play a game in Yankee Stadium? What about a basketball player playing in Madison Square Garden or a football player stepping foot onto Lambeau Field in Green Bay?

All this fighting between the owners and the players has to stop. It has to stop for the good of all sports. If it doesn't, they're gonna stick a stake right through the heart of what makes all of our games so great for so many people.

I recently read an article on Muhammad Ali. He said: "Life is too short for you to ever waste on hatred." You can apply that to everything. You can't have hatred between the owners and players. Both sides have to share the pie.

When they're slicing up that pie, though, they better remember who put it on the table for them. And that's every mother, father, and child who walks into that park.

If the players think they own this game, I've got news for them. If the owners think they own this game, they better listen up, too.

Yes, the players are the showcase. They're the ones who write the history books and deserve whatever their salaries are because the owners are willing to pay. Yes, the owners own the teams. You can look it up in the records and their names will show up on the deeds.

But neither side owns the game. It don't matter what sport you're talking about. The game belongs to the fans. All we do is lease it.

We lease it by the way we treat the fans. We must respect every single person who comes to see us play.

When kids ask me for my autograph, I always sign and return the item with a "thank you." I hear them ask their daddy, "How come he says 'thank you' when he signs a ball?" I thank them for asking. They're only showing respect for the game.

Owners must understand that the game revolves around great players. Without great players, all the owners have is money. But without the people, nobody has nothing. If you've got the greatest talent in the world and you ain't got nobody in the stands to watch that talent play, what do you have?

If we lose contact with the fans—and that's what we've done—you're headed to El Paso and you ain't got no horse.

Fans ain't fools. They ain't coming to throw their dollars into the kitty when all they get is a big laugh. Let me tell you, they're smart enough to put that last laugh on you.

We might be seeing some of that change in minor league baseball today. Look at all the franchises that are drawing record numbers of people to the park. Mom and Pop can afford those tickets. Players there go out and bust their behinds. That's what the game really is about.

It's supposed to be fun. And what's wrong with having fun?

I still get letters congratulating me on my decision. Everybody doesn't agree. I just hope people will finally understand exactly why I did what I had to do.

When I look back at that time, I'm more proud of

what I did than anything else I've done in the game. The record books will take care of themselves. I had to prove to myself I could stand up and be counted.

To this day I thank God I did.

I know in my heart I have nothing else to prove. I kept my class. It wasn't for sale then and never will be in the future.

That's a feeling no amount of money can buy. If a principle has a price tag on it, you better pass it by.

SPARKY

Only a handful of America's superstar celebrities and athletes enjoy first-name identity.

The club is restricted exclusively to the nation's most celebrated. Members are carefully selected by the public. Membership is not for sale, so all celebrities need not apply.

Everyone recognizes Oprah . . . Madonna . . . Muhammad . . . Elvis . . . "The Babe."

The young Tiger may not yet enjoy such universal recognition. But at least he's identified even by those who don't religiously follow sports.

Living in that exclusive neighborhood provides special privilege. That privilege, however, is accompanied by a proportionately larger public responsibility.

Sparky has reached such single-name celebrity status. Not everyone knows him. But even those not familiar with baseball history, somewhere someplace at least have heard the name.

When the nickname was born, Sparky wasn't exactly excited over its connotation. He embraced the tag only after its attachment became inevitably permanent.

The name is a natural. It fits more snugly than "Rocky" on a fighter.

Sparky is a peppery little guy with more spunk than talent. He's as bubbly as a shaken bottle of warm soda. Even at sixty-four, he's a hurricane of energy. His biggest problem is not knowing how to sit still. He's more animated than a Disney cartoon.

Sparky's propensity for one-word answers is about the same as for a presidential hopeful during a campaign speech.

It simply does not exist.

Sparky speaks in stories, often creating his own words. Those that he chooses are spit out like BB pellets. They're fired randomly. Sports writers often do double takes trying to decipher exactly what they're hearing.

Some of his malapropisms have assumed lives of their own. Once when describing a young player whose well-defined muscles suggested the power of Babe Ruth, Sparky commented to the writers: "He looks like a Greek goddess."

Another time in the heat of a pennant race when a writer asked Sparky about some injured players on his team, he defiantly answered: "Pain don't hurt."

There was one spring training when Sparky kept referring to the "zifarod" of his team. It was a totally concocted word that supposedly measured the spirit of the team compared to its actual physical talents.

It also was designed to spark a little fun. Sparky's look on life is simple—"nothing ain't worth nothing if you can't have a few laughs."

Sparky's bent for humor is accompanied by a genuine concern for people. Greater than his gift for gab is the sort of down-home respect he extends to every person he meets.

When first tagged with the 'Sparky' handle, though, he felt embarrassed by its connotation.

"I thought it was a name for a dog or some comic strip character," Sparky recalled.

Over the years, of course, he's reconciled Sparky with the real George Anderson. Although the two remain as distinct as Abbott and Costello, they have blended beautifully to create one of contemporary America's truly colorful characters.

And more important than the amusement he has provided a nation is the goodwill he has generated both in and out of the game of baseball.

The difference between Sparky and George is similar to Sean Connery and his alter ego, James Bond. While Connery always carries the Bond mystique, Sparky is, in fact, part of the real George Anderson.

So he always makes certain that the character conducts himself with class.

The name itself was created in 1955 by a radio announcer who broadcasted the Class AA games at Fort Worth, Texas. Sparky was playing his third professional season and had developed a reputation for his fiery brand of ball. After yet another argument with an umpire, the radio man innocently reported, "the sparks are really flying tonight."

"Sparks" transformed to "Sparky" and the name stuck. The character was created and Sparky carefully rode it to heights George never could have imagined.

"Spar-kay, Spar-kay . . . give me one ball, please, Sparkay," French-Canadian fans would implore him when he played in Montreal as a minor leaguer.

Even though the name quickly became firmly attached, Sparky still signed autographs "George Anderson" during his first year as manager of Cincinnati in 1970. Until the Reds' publicity department asked him to switch to "Sparky," he almost downplayed the identity.

The emerging character had other distinguishing marks that refused to let Anderson remain the anonymous baseball figure he thought he would always remain.

In spite of being only thirty-five years old when named manager of the Reds, his black hair turned to snowy white after only a few seasons at the helm. Coupled with his chiseled bronze face from years of playing in the sun, Sparky stands out in a crowd like a nudist in a monastery.

For Sparky, there's never a place to hide.

From the shoulder-to-shoulder sidewalks of New York to the sleepy bayous of Baton Rouge, Louisiana, Sparky is as anonymous as a Fourth of July parade.

Two other factors clinched Sparky's permanent departure from obscurity. First it was the Reds who, under Sparky in the '70s, developed into baseball's last legitimate dynasty. And to top it off, Sparky learned to handle and actually enjoy his newly found freedom of being able to mount a soapbox almost at will.

"He's so doggone recognizable," said former major league catcher Pete Daley. He and Sparky played briefly together in the minor leagues. Now they play golf together regularly in Thousand Oaks, California where Sparky lives.

"He's just got that special look about him and he's been exposed to the national media so much that everybody knows who he is," Daley added. "You can pass some big stars on the street and walk right by without noticing them. Not Sparky. He's like Michael Jordan or Magic Johnson."

People love to hear Sparky talk. And Sparky never finds himself at a loss for a few thousand words.

"After I went to the Tigers as a coach in 1979, I'll never forget the moment we walked off the plane in Detroit," said Billy Consolo who has known Sparky since both were twelve years old.

"There must have been 200 writers and radio and TV people. My jaw dropped to the floor. Not just from the number of reporters, but also by the way George handled it."

Sparky's conversations often start with only a handful of people around. Usually it's with an ordinary worker such as a cab driver or baggage handler in an airport. Before he's into his second well-chosen sentence, Sparky's court has grown to a crowd. And his dialogue grows in proportion.

Amazingly, Sparky was painfully shy until his avalanche of public recognition.

"When we were kids, neither one of us could talk in front of more than two people," Consolo explained. "When he was with Cincinnati and came home during off-seasons, we were always around friends so I never paid much attention. Now when he talks to a group of writers or is on some national television show, he's always in control. The way he talks sometimes gives me goose bumps."

There's a magnetism about Sparky that instinctively commands attention.

"Right after our first season in Detroit, he and I went to Las Vegas for a television show he was going to shoot," Consolo recalled. "There was a big casino floor directly opposite the front desk. When we walked into that hotel, some of the people playing the slot machines spotted him with that white hair. All of a sudden people started saying, 'Sparky, Sparky, Sparky.'

"I said to myself, I can't believe what I'm seeing. Here we

are in Las Vegas with all the glitz and lights and action, and people actually stopped just to get George to wave at them."

The entertainment Mecca doesn't have a lock on Sparky's popularity. Even New York's Wall Street took a second look.

Before a night game at Yankee Stadium when he was managing the Tigers, Sparky visited the New York Stock Exchange accompanied by Hall of Famer George Kell and former Tiger boss Jim Campbell.

"I had never been there," Campbell said. "All the commotion was enough to make you dizzy. People were running, shouting, waving their arms.

"I couldn't believe it. As soon as some of those brokers spotted Sparky, they quit what they were doing and came over to shake his hand. I said to myself, 'Well, I'll be a son of a gun. Here we are in one of the most powerful buildings in America and these guys who are dealing in millions of dollars want to shake this little guy's hand.'"

Even in Manhattan where crowded sidewalks turn pedestrians into bumper cars, walking the streets with Sparky is an adventure. Everyone seems to recognize him. Although it's only a brief encounter, Sparky tries to acknowledge all with a handshake, a few quick words or at least a smile.

"Hey, Spah-kee," a passer-by says while extending his hand.

"When you gonna manage the Yankees, Spah-kee?" asks another.

"Give me an autograph, Spah-kee," cries another.

Sparky remains accommodating to the point of his own inconvenience. This vigilant concern for others is always guaranteed under the watchful eye of George.

Sparky's daughter, Shirlee, embraces a lesson she learned from her father after the Tigers had won the World Series in 1984. Back home in Thousand Oaks, the two were waiting in line for service at the bank.

"There was a long line and all the people wanted to talk to my dad," Shirlee recalled. "He was telling stories and signing autographs when a teller spotted my father and waved for him to come up to the front. I'll never forget it. He smiled and thanked her, but said he'd wait his turn.

"If he had walked to the front of that line, I would have been so disappointed in him. I'm one of those people who would have been standing in that line. I don't care who it is. Nobody deserves special treatment like that.

"I think to this day, he's still amazed that people notice him. He enjoys it, but he never abuses it. That's what I'm really proud of him for."

Sparky has made his share of mistakes. Early in his career, his temper on the field was a land mine just waiting to be tickled. Memories never made with his children because of his workaholic personality still haunt him.

Overall, however, while Sparky remains the closest baseball showman to the legendary Casey Stengel, George remains the guy next door. He was raised in the belief that no one person is better than another. He never compromises his respect for other people.

Sparky is show business. He's a technicolor action figure who is always the star of the film. George is the black-and-white everybody who enjoys most evenings on the normal side of TV.

During his career, Sparky has visited with three Presidents of the United States, countless celebrated entertainers and almost every popular athlete and coach. He's even met the Pope.

Sparky is honored by the opportunities he never dreamed he would have. But he receives the same amount of enjoyment from swapping stories with the barber, the bellman, or anybody he happens to meet who just wants to talk a little bit about life.

Position makes no difference to Sparky. In fact, he has no clue of how to make that differentiation.

When he was managing in the major leagues, a cab driver, a plumber, or a waiter was as likely to wind up sitting in Sparky's box in the stands as was the president of Ford Motor Company.

"There are so many things I learned from the man," said Hall of Fame second baseman Joe Morgan who played for Sparky with the Reds.

"He always said, when you walk into a room, speak to

everybody. It doesn't take anything to say hello. It doesn't cost you anything to smile. I think in this day and age, that's not a normal occurrence. Sparky always said you can disarm anybody if you walk into a room and smile. I can't say I do it all the time, but I try. I carry that from Sparky."

During the glory years of the Reds, Sparky was walking to New York's Shea Stadium after a subway ride from the hotel. He spotted Terry and Ray Murphy, a recently married young couple, scurrying across a parking lot toward the park.

"Where are you two kids running to?" Sparky initiated the conversation.

"We're going to see The Big Red Machine," the young Mrs. Murphy replied. "We just love them."

Suddenly she stopped and stared in total disbelief at the stranger.

"Aren't you . . . ?" she incredulously asked.

"Yes, I happen to be that person," Sparky replied, almost apologetically. "But there ain't no tickets left for The Big Red Machine. This game's been sold out for weeks."

The young lady nearly cried.

"But I'm gonna tell you what I'm gonna do," Sparky continued. "You're gonna give me your name and I'm gonna leave tickets for you in my box. But you have to promise not to boo me tonight no matter what kind of dumb move I might make."

The Murphys never forgot their stroke of fortune. To this day, they send birthday and Christmas cards to Sparky and Carol. And simply because Sparky spent a few moments just being nice.

"I learned more from being around Sparky than anybody I've been around in my life," said Pete Rose. "He's nice to everybody. You really have to crap all over Sparky for him not to be nice to you."

Being Sparky hasn't always been easy. Trying to walk in the safety of the shadows is difficult when the spotlight is always shining. It takes a special person.

Sparky . . . no other name is needed.

What Are You Doing Here?

A few years ago during the off-season when I managed the Tigers, I pulled into my garage after a trip to the Thrifty Drug Store a few blocks from home in Thousand Oaks.

A car pulled up and parked in front of my driveway. There were two men I didn't recognize. I walked up to the car and asked if I could help.

"I live up the road in Newbury Park," the driver said.

"I'm out here visiting from Lansing, Michigan," the passenger said. "I'm a big Tiger fan and I heard you lived in the area. We saw you coming out of the store and I wanted to see where you live."

We talked a little about the Tigers. I told them how much I loved the whole state of Michigan. I told him I had even visited Lansing a few times.

"Home of the Michigan State Spartans," I joked with him. "I follow your football team."

After a few minutes, they were getting ready to leave.

"I'm a little disappointed," the man from Michigan said.

"Why is that, sir?" I asked.

"Because I thought you lived in a much nicer house," he answered.

They took off and I went inside and told my wife, Carol, what happened. To this day, I still can't figure out just what kind of house I'm supposed to live in. I always thought a home is what you make of it. Carol and me are pretty happy, so I hope I ain't disappointing too many people.

I understood what that man meant. Sparky is supposed to live in some fancy fenced-off mansion with a swimming pool. He's supposed to have a Mercedes. I'd be afraid to drive something that expensive. I'll just stick with my Probe.

Me and Carol built this house in 1967. We couldn't afford anything closer to Los Angeles. It took a few years before we could even afford the furniture.

It's the only house we've owned. It's the only one we'll ever own. We probably could buy something a little bigger or a little more fancy.

But why? This is where we're happy. This is home. Every time I pull out of my driveway, I take a look back at it just to remind myself how lucky we've been.

I know I'm the real Sparky. But Sparky ain't the real me. Not the one way down deep inside.

It's something like a Christmas present. George is the gift that's wrapped up inside the box. Sparky is the ribbons and bows that make the gift look pretty.

Well, let me tell you something . . . if what's inside the box ain't nothing but a piece of garbage, then all the fancy trimming can't make it good.

No matter which way you look at it, it's always still the same. A pig is still a pig even if you pour a bottle of perfume on it. And Cinderella is still gonna be pretty even if she's wearing a potato sack. The bottom line is always the same—it's what's inside that counts.

We have a funny thing going on here in America. For whatever reason—and I ain't exactly sure why—we put athletes and celebrities somewhere up on top of a mountain and treat them better than we do most other people.

Just because they're up there on top of that mountain, that don't make them no better than anybody else. They're a lot more fortunate, but they ain't no better.

Look around at any sport. Look at Tiger Woods right now. He's the biggest thing to come along since they put red in lipstick. He's a wonderful golfer. He might wind up being the best we ever knew. I never met him so I don't know what kind of kid he is. He might be marvelous. But I'll tell you one thing for sure—he ain't no better than any other kid anywhere.

There's a lot of people in the world that are more fortunate than others. But I guarantee you God never made one person who is better than anybody else.

Every person God created is the most important person on this earth. If he wasn't the most important, then why did God waste His time making him in the first place?

God's got more important things to worry about than making Jimmy better than Judy or Sally better than Tom.

I ain't no better than anybody else. I have been fortunate. And for that, Sparky has played a big part.

I know the difference between Sparky and George. And there were times when I was disappointed with the way Sparky acted.

There were times, particularly after losses, when I acted like a spoiled little rich kid who wanted all the toys. I honestly used to think that Sparky was never supposed to lose. Losing was for all the other managers. Sparky was supposed to be special.

I'll never forgive myself for the night when I was managing Cincinnati and I left my parents in the parking lot after the Dodgers had whipped us. That really took a lot of brains. They shouldda told me they didn't care to see me anyway.

Thank God, George was able to jump in before Sparky ran too far out of control.

People always want to do things for Sparky. Not let

him wait to be seated in a restaurant or give him things just because he's him.

When you think about it, that don't make no sense. But if you feed somebody enough candy, I guarantee you that guy will end up with a sweet tooth.

If it wasn't for George, who knows how much candy Sparky might have gobbled up?

For instance, I've seen people make a scene in a restaurant or yell at somebody carrying his bags. That waitress in the restaurant could be your sister or your mother. That bellman carrying your bags could just as easily be your brother. What makes those people any less than everybody else?

When a person is blessed with being what we call a celebrity, that person has a tougher job than everybody else. He's got an obligation to make everyone he meets feel good about meeting him. If he don't, then shame on him because he's the one who has been blessed.

I remember a fancy party where I was dressed in a tux with tails. Carol was all dressed up in some fancy gown. Rod Dedeaux, the old USC baseball coach, introduced us to a lady as Georgie and Carol Anderson. The lady stuck out her hand and quickly walked away.

Ten minutes later, I heard her shout from across the room—"Why didn't you tell me you were Sparky Anderson?"

I got so upset, I wanted to stick those tails inside my belt and get out of that place faster than my feet could run. Carol was angry, too, but she kept her cool. She convinced me not to make a scene.

Was I any kind of different person just because I was Sparky? You mean all of a sudden in ten minutes I got more important because I was the manager of a big league team?

A manager ain't no more important than a cab driver. A president of a company ain't no better than the factory worker who works for him.

I'm very grateful for what Sparky has done for me and my family. He's been good to us and good for the game. But I do know the difference between Sparky and the real me.

Sparky is show business. He's never met a camera he didn't like. He's never left a reporter's notebook empty. He can talk to a stranger sitting in a restaurant or he can get up on a stage and start yapping like one of those TV preachers.

In fact, there ain't a time when Sparky's not on stage.

Sparky is the character that helped get me through 26 big league seasons. When he was in those five World Series, nobody had more fun than him.

I thank Sparky for the way he's helped me and my family. Without him, George would have turned into stone sitting in front of the TV set. Sparky is fun. George is such a bore his shadow is afraid to come out.

I remember one time I was in the Burger King. A stranger acted surprised to see Sparky there.

"Why do you come to the Burger King?" he asked.

I guess he figured Sparky was always supposed to eat at some fancy restaurant.

"Because I like them," I answered.

When I was with the Tigers in spring training one year, Ted Williams was a batting instructor for the Red Sox. During batting practice before an exhibition game in Winter Haven, I spotted him near the Boston dugout.

I was walking over to say hello when he stuck out his hand and said, "Hi, I'm Ted Williams."

My jaw must have dropped to the shoestrings on my spikes.

"There might be somebody living under a rock somewhere in Borneo who don't know who you are, but everybody else knows you're the greatest hitter that ever lived," I told him.

"There might be someone who doesn't," Williams

said. "I don't ever want to make him feel embarrassed for not knowing who I am."

He taught me a lesson that I'll never forget. Whenever I meet anybody for the first time, I always introduce myself and then call that person by his or her name.

That person is a human being. He deserves that respect. Just because he might not be a celebrity don't make him anything less than I am. I'm pretty sure when you check in at those pearly gates, all those newspaper clippings ain't gonna get you a better spot.

One of my favorite days of the year is Thanksgiving. All the old guys who went to Dorsey High get together for a touch football game at the old playground.

There are doctors, lawyers, plumbers, painters. Even Howard Weitzman shows up. He's one of L.A.'s most famous lawyers. Some of his clients were Michael Jackson and O.J. Simpson.

That might be big in the courts. But at the Turkey Bowl, he's just little Howard Weitzman. Around these guys, he's just one of the old guys from Dorsey. And he better not drop no passes either.

I'm just plain old George there. In fact, I'm not too sure some of the guys even know Sparky is around.

That's the way it's supposed to be. That's the way I like it best.

Nobody better than nobody else. Only some a little more fortunate than others.

I hope some of our younger stars and all young people learn that lesson before it's too late. They might find out they can be a whole lot happier.

Sparky and George did.

Makers of Men

Sparky quickly credits players for his record-setting managerial success.

Without the horses, there simply is no race.

All truly successful leaders follow a similar path. The inspiring school principal quickly acknowledges the dedication of the entire faculty. The manager of a busy bank can't generate new business without the reliability of the tellers at the windows. The shift foreman in an automobile plant might wind up with three wheels and two steering columns without cooperation from the hourly workers who put all the pieces together.

In baseball, though, sometimes the most talented teams never make it into October. For one reason or another, the challenge of the season is surrendered to the weakness of the moment.

Sometimes even the best don't know how to finish the race.

Sometimes players just can't finish a successful season after leading all the way. Often, the responsibility falls squarely on the manager. He's the one everyone looks to for that one last push up the final hill.

"There's a difference between a good manager and a great one," said Cincinnati Hall of Fame catcher Johnny Bench. "The good one will tell you there's more than one way to skin a cat. The great manager will convince the cat it's necessary. Sparky had the cats carrying the knives to him."

Sparky was the best at riding a good team to the finish line. When he had the chance to win, he never let it slip away. When he smelled blood, no shark was quicker to the kill.

"It doesn't matter what sport or business you're talking about," said Bo Schembechler, the former Tiger president who is a football coaching legend at the University of Michigan.

"The best manager or coach can't make a bad team good. But if that same guy has a good team, just watch him operate when the clock is running down. He'll bring that team to the finish line like a thoroughbred running against a pack of mules. That was Sparky. He owned the finish line."

Baseball is more than hitting and running and pitching. Like any other walk of life, people define its essence. People dictate results on the field. How those people operate is the responsibility of the manager.

Running the game between the foul lines is the easiest part of the job. Preparing the players to expend all their talent and energy separates the good manager from the also-rans.

It doesn't take a genius to be a successful baseball manager. It does, however, take a leader to develop a group of gifted athletes as players and men.

Bench, for instance, would have carved his own Hall of Fame career even if he had played for Bozo the Clown. It wouldn't have mattered who the manager had been.

Without Sparky, however, Bench admits he wouldn't be the man he is today.

Sparky was tireless to his commitment. To succeed as a manager, he had to develop talent. To excel as a leader, he had to help each individual develop as a man.

"Sparky would have been a helluva psychiatrist," said Pete Rose. "That's what managing is. It doesn't matter what field it is. It's amazing how people try to run their businesses and don't know their personnel.

"Sparky knew his personnel. He always knew who he could put into a situation where they might fail and it wouldn't bother them. They were kind of kick-ass guys and were up for the challenge. Other people can't be put into a situation where they're going to fail because they'll fail every damn time. Sparky knew the difference."

Rose explained that Sparky had a simple philosophy for handling players.

"You can kick a guy in the ass . . . you can pat him on the ass . . . or you can leave him alone," Rose said. "Sparky didn't kick a guy that needed patting and he didn't pat those that needed kicking. And he didn't do either one to guys who just needed to be left alone.

"I played for 11 managers. Sparky was the best at knowing his people. Managers in all kinds of other businesses can learn a lesson from Sparky."

One of Sparky's finest jobs of kicking occurred while he managed the Tigers. He knew he had one of the brightest pieces of young raw talent in the game with Kirk Gibson.

Gibson exploded on the scene as baseball's golden boy. He was the hometown hero who had more natural athletic ability than Madonna has sex appeal.

Gibson had been an All-American football wide receiver for Michigan State University. He was good enough to be considered a National Football League can't-miss superstar prospect.

He also was an All-American in baseball. He rewrote all of the school's hitting records. He smashed balls over the Red Cedar River. Scouting reports said he could outrun his shadow.

Gibson was the Tigers' No. 1 draft pick. Shortly after arriving in the major leagues, he was hailed as the next Mickey Mantle.

Gibson showed flashes of brilliance during his first four years. Off the field, though, he was as much a heartbreaking bust as he was spectacular on the diamond.

Gibson simply refused to mature as a person. Gibson, admittedly, had made life difficult for all those around him. He was surly and self-centered. His outlook on life crippled his development as a player.

A showdown between Sparky and his malcontent would-be superstar was inevitable. It came crashing down the day before the 1983 season opener in Minnesota.

Sparky told Gibson he would not be in the starting lineup for the first game against the Twins. Furthermore, he no longer was an automatic starter. He would be platooned based upon the opposing starting pitcher.

"You've been acting like an idiot," Sparky told him.

Gibson was devastated. No one had ever stood up to him like that. He threatened to break his little manager in half. But the decision had been made. Sparky was not about to waver.

"I went through a period of my life where my priorities were mis-aligned," Gibson admitted. "I wasn't focused on what I was there for.

"Sparky didn't like what he saw in me as a person. In '83, he took a stance on me. He played me every day my first four years, almost to the point of pampering me. I think he finally said to himself, 'O.K., I tried it one way. Now I've got to try something else. This kid is at a point in his life where he could really go the wrong way as a baseball player and as a person.'"

Sparky's decision took guts. The Tigers had invested a lot of money in Gibson. More than money, they also had invested their future. If the Tigers were truly going to develop into champions, Gibson was expected to play an integral part.

After watching his would-be superstar both on and off the field, Sparky knew Gibson wasn't headed anywhere except smack into a brick wall at the dead end of the street.

The decision had been made and it was final. Until further notice, Gibson's position was on the bench. The bold move was bound to draw a lot of criticism. Sparky didn't care.

He knew it was the right thing to do.

Sparky ran the risk of losing a potential superstar. But he preferred giving up the player to losing the man inside.

Sparky stuck to his plan to help Gibson gain his maturity. He kept the lines of communication open for any time Gibson wanted to tune in.

Before a game in Seattle, Gibson and his best friend, pitcher Dave Rozema, were running in the outfield. Sparky wandered out to center and teased Gibson by lining up as a defensive back. Despite Gibson's overpowering size advantage, Sparky dared him to slip by for an imaginary pass.

Gibson not only took the dare, he seized the opportunity for a slice of misguided revenge. First, he flashed Sparky a head fake. On his way by, he shot a forearm to Sparky's chest that sent the little manager flying. When he finally hit the ground, Sparky rolled over three times and looked up at Rozema with water in his eyes.

"That S.O.B. is crazy," Sparky said to Rozema.

"Which S.O.B. is crazy?" Gibson looked down at Sparky. "The guy who ran over you or the guy who lined up in front of this bulldozer?"

Sparky got up and straightened his shirt.

"You'll find out who the boss is around here," Sparky barked. "And it ain't you."

Sparky was physically sore for the next few days. But the lesson hit Gibson hardest. Sparky delivered it in the language that Gibson understood best.

"I was upset because I wasn't playing," Gibson said. "But he didn't bury me for that. He understood. It was his way of making sure we kept our dialogue going.

"He sacrificed for me. I hammered him. It was his way of saying—go ahead . . . you're frustrated . . . let me have it . . . I don't care . . . but I'm here with you like I told you . . . you're the idiot . . . you're going down the wrong road . . . you're going to sit your ass on the bench till you get the picture.

"When it was all said and done, Sparky wanted me and all of us to be proud of what we did in the game and be proud of ourselves as persons. That's the definition of Sparky Anderson."

Most lessons Sparky imparted to his players were accompanied with less physical pain.

"He's street-smart," Rose said. "He reads people like a book and treats everybody as an individual.

"For instance, in spring training, nobody plays every game. Sparky knew I love basketball. When the NCAA finals came around, he knew I had a special interest in them. On

Saturdays, he let me do my work early and then go home to watch the games.

"Johnny Bench and Joe Morgan loved to play golf. There were a lot of tournaments in spring training and he'd let them go play after their work was done. What's the difference which day you take off in spring training?"

Sparky told the rest of the players when they had accomplished all of the things that some of his stars had, they'd receive the same considerations.

"He knew the value of keeping guys happy," Rose said. "We never took advantage of him. He wouldn't allow it."

Sparky's approach to managing stretched far beyond the ballpark. Everyone knew how well Rose and Bench and Morgan and Tony Perez and Dave Concepcion could play for the Reds. The same was true for Gibson and Alan Trammell and Lou Whitaker and Lance Parrish on the Tigers. Sparky's concern also extended to how well they developed off the field.

"We were at the Detroit writers' dinner one night when I received the Tiger of the Year award," Gibson recalled. "Sparky made a comment about the responsibility players have to sign autographs and treat people right. He didn't say my name. He didn't have to. I got the picture. That's how he was. He had a sincere interest in every guy he touched. He gave you a chance to share his knowledge. Part of my development came because Sparky refused to quit. He stressed becoming a man all the time."

Part of Sparky's approach was getting to know each player and each player's family.

"When he made a trade for somebody, he already knew if the guy could hit or pitch," Rose said. "Any bozo could figure that out. Sparky took the time to get to know the guy personally. He got to know the wives and all the kids. I don't care if you're a baseball manager or the president of some company. You can get so much more out of a guy if you just take time to show him that you care."

Controlling the clubhouse was always Sparky's main concern. If the clubhouse was under control, the field would take care of itself.

"You know how people always refer to Vince Lombardi as 'Coach'?" Trammell said. "That's the way I think of Sparky.

"He knew his players inside and out. It amazed me how he could get the most out of all 25 guys year after year. Even when times were tough, it was a comfort when Sparky walked into the clubhouse. You knew things were under control then. There was never any chaos in Sparky's clubhouse. He was like a father figure.

"He taught us the importance of conducting ourselves like professionals. He taught us the importance of dressing properly on the road and cooperating with the media. All those little things add up to make the total person. More than anything else, he taught us how to treat people the way we wanted to be treated. I raise my kids the way Sparky helped to raise me."

Managing a baseball team or a line in the automobile factory, the principles remain the same.

Sparky just happened to do his managing in a baseball cap and knickers.

TAKE THE TIME

Early in my career when I was with Cincinnati, we had a pitcher named Jim McGlothlin. He was a marvelous young man. He was a good family man and was good with all his teammates. He had a pretty good year in 1970.

In spring training the next year, I noticed he wasn't running so good. I called over my pitching coach, Larry Shepard.

"You tell that S.O.B. to get with it," I told him. "When he's doing his running, I expect him to run."

A few years later, Jimmy died of cancer.

I'm not sure what happened to him in spring training, but I think he must have been tired. And I never took the time to find out why. I couldn't have saved his life. But I certainly could have been there to understand his problem.

These are some of the things that all young people have to think about. If you don't ever take the time to really find out about the people in your life, then you don't know them at all. You're not doing a good job and you're not being a good person.

I've always been pretty good at reading people. But I messed up that time. After that incident, I promised myself never to let anything like that happen again.

It's not the player's responsibility to get to know the manager. It's the manager's job to get to know his players—on the field and off.

It's not the worker's job to get to know the boss. The

boss has to take the lead to know his workers—in the office or the factory and away.

When I was a young player coming up in the minor leagues, I never could understand why a manager would give the same speech year after year. It didn't matter what team or what league. It was always the same old story—we didn't have to like the manager, but we had to respect him.

What a bunch of baloney!

The first part made sense. Maybe I didn't like him. But how was I supposed to respect him if he wasn't worth a dirty dime? Nobody ain't gonna get my respect if they don't earn it.

Every spring training, I gave my teams a little different talk. I told them they didn't have to like me. And furthermore, they didn't have to respect me. If I didn't earn their respect, why in the hell were they supposed to?

It's the same thing with parents who lay the same trick on their kids. Maybe the parents are derelicts. Maybe they go around drinking and lying and cheating. Now they want their kids to respect them just because they're their parents.

Get serious!

You can't tell those kids how to act right. You have to show them. You can't demand respect. You have to earn it. Words don't get it. Only the action counts.

Maybe it's us grown-ups that have to set our priorities straight so that we can help the kids. Let's don't tell them one thing and then run behind the curtains and do something else.

Managing a baseball team is no different than managing any group of people in any kind of job. People are people. They gotta be treated with dignity. I don't care if a guy's hitting fourth in the lineup or delivering mail. As long as that man is doing the best job he can, then he should be treated with dignity and respect.

It's the manager's job to understand what each player can and can't do. If a player can't hit the long ball, that ain't his fault. Don't embarrass him and hurt your team trying to get him to swing for the fences because he just can't do it.

If little Johnny just can't get the hang of playing baseball or football or soccer, it ain't no good for his parents to stand there and scream at him. Take the time to find out what little Johnny really wants to do.

Johnny might have some other kind of talent. He wants to be good. We have to take time to help him find his talent and develop it.

The only way a manager is gonna truly find out about his players is by taking the time to get to know them. He's got to figure out which guys to joke with and which ones to leave alone.

For instance, when I was talking to a religious kid, I never used no swear words. If I was talking to a street kid, I talked his talk and told him stories that wanted to make him get down on his knees and beg for forgiveness before he left my office. And if I was dealing with a young man who was a little afraid of me, I made it real gentle and quiet. It was my job to make him know that I understood how he was feeling.

I used to tell my players, "You might think you're a pretty good con man, but you don't want no part of this cat. I put the 'C' in con." I don't mean that in no negative way. I just knew I could tap dance in every situation.

I wasn't pulling no con job when I tried to learn about everybody's family, though. I was dead serious about that. I always made a point of learning about a player's wife and the names of all his kids.

If you're gonna spend most of the year with a guy, shouldn't you know something about his family? What if that man runs into a little problem? You're supposed to be there to lend a helping hand.

Pete Rose used to tell me he could never trick me

when something was bothering him. I could read it on his face as soon as he walked into the clubhouse. He didn't have to say a word.

By the time he came to talk to me, I already knew that something was wrong and I had to try to help.

That's something you get from knowing the people around you. Even if you don't say nothing, they know that you're there in case they want to talk.

Every player comes from a different environment. Every player has a different kind of parents and different kind of home. It was my responsibility to figure that out. If I understood them, I could basically deal with almost any kind of problem.

I'll never forget one time when I was managing Rock Hill in 1965. We were playing a game in Greenville, South Carolina.

I had a young black outfielder named Bobby Boss on my team. Bobby was not a great baseball player. It was obvious he was not gonna move up the ladder and play at a high level.

But he was such a great person. His parents had done such a wonderful job with him.

We stopped the bus at a little restaurant before going to the park. We grabbed a bunch of tables and the lady came over to get our order.

She asked who the manager was and I told her it was me. She asked if I could step aside to speak with her privately.

"I can serve all you guys except that colored boy over there," she said.

I remained calm for a second, which was an upset for me.

"Well, what is he supposed to do?" I asked her.

"He'll have to eat on the bus," she said.

To this day, I don't know how I kept myself from tearing the whole place up. I settled on telling her she could take all her food and shove it some place I knew she would never dream of doing.

"There ain't nobody gonna eat here if he can't eat here," I told her.

I took the whole team and got back on the bus. I was still boiling 20 miles down the highway.

After a little while, Bobby came up and very quietly asked if he could sit by me for a minute. He was almost crying.

"Skip, I'm so sorry that I caused this problem," he said.

I remember grabbing his arm.

"Bobby, you're gonna live a lot of years," I told him. "You and me can't solve ignorance. We can only act the way God meant us to act. But let me tell you something—you have done nothing to cause this. You always remember to do the right thing. That lady better say her prayers tonight because I know that ain't the way God wants us to treat each other."

If Bobby never learned anything about baseball, I know that he learned something a whole lot more important.

I don't know what Bobby is doing now. Whatever it is, I'm sure he's doing all right. He was raised by good parents and was a terrific kid. Some of the lessons he had to learn, unfortunately, came the hard way. But I know he's a better man for it today.

These are the things that are far more important than all the games. And the only way a manager is gonna be able to deal with all of them is by taking the time to really know his players.

That's what makes the difference between a good teacher and an average one. The good ones let their students know they really care about what they make of their lives. If an "A" student gets a "B" on a test, the good teacher is gonna let that student know he's disappointed. If a "C" student is failing, the good teacher is gonna step in before that student doesn't pass the course.

It's the same thing at work. The good boss ain't satisfied with just getting the job done. He makes sure all his workers feel appreciated. If it takes a little extra time and effort, that's why he's the boss.

Winning is a manager's first responsibility. He owes that to his owner. He owes that to his team. And he owes that to the fans. But he's also got to teach his young men how to become better fathers and better citizens.

If a manager don't do that, then shame on him. He's only doing half his job and it ain't the half that's more important.

That same principle applies to all walks of life. It's impossible to be the best at any job if you're only half a man.

If a young man or woman learns how to conduct themselves properly and how to do the right thing, that don't mean they're gonna be a better player or a better worker. But they will become better persons. And in the long run, ain't that a better measure than all the wins and losses?

I've seen a lot of players come along in this game who have a lot of talent. They want to be good. They want to enjoy all the rewards that go with it. But they just won't sweat and make the sacrifice it takes to reach the top. I call them "wanna-be's." They wind up being "never-wases."

I think the worst thing anybody can have written on their tombstone is that "he had potential."

The lights always seem to be a little brighter in sports, but it doesn't matter which path a person chooses to follow in life. If a person fails to live up to his potential, he might as well not jump into the game in the first place.

It doesn't matter how much or how little ability any individual has. It's up to that individual to get the most out of whatever it is. And it's up to the leader—whether he's the manager, coach, boss, parent, or teacher—to help coax that potential to rise to the top.

Not only as a player or professional, but also as the total person.

Little Georgie Is Still the Same

Sparky's fascination with people got an early start. Besides baseball, basketball, and whatever other kind of competition that offered a challenge, nothing grabbed Sparky's interest more as a youth than simply watching other people.

From ever since he can remember, he was fascinated by everything people did around him. Family, friends, even strangers.

"There were times when I was with my mama that she would accidentally walk off without me because I got lost just staring at people," Sparky recalled.

"I wondered why they all seemed to hurry around so much. I wondered where they were going and what they did for a living. I played all kinds of games in my mind."

Sparky's formal education stopped after high school. But as Pete Rose describes him, he turned himself into "one of the wisest street-smart people" he ever met.

Sparky was born George Lee Anderson on February 22, 1934 in Bridgewater, South Dakota. It would be many years before little Georgie would develop into Sparky.

With his father LeRoy, mother Shirley, brother Bill and sisters Beverly, Carolyn, and Sharon, he lived in a two-story frame house that had no bathroom and a coal stove in the living room. It got so cold in the winter that LeRoy had to paste cardboard over all the windows to keep the heat from running off into those frigid Dakota nights.

LeRoy scuffled week to week to pay all the bills. He

painted silos and farmhouses. He also delivered mail to earn a few extra dollars.

In his spare time, LeRoy played catcher on the Bridgewater semipro baseball team. He loved the sport and played catch with little Georgie every chance he got. To help develop Georgie's arm, in the winter he made his son throw baseballs into a pillow on the bed.

Georgie learned the game early by serving as batboy for his father's team. It also gave him the chance to work out with more experienced players. Even at that young age, Georgie sensed he could always learn a lot of things from people who "had been there."

Mother Shirley was always concerned about Georgie's schoolwork. Brother Bill never posed such a problem. He was a good student who later became a teacher after graduating from UCLA.

"Georgie, how come Billy has so many books and you never bring any home," his mother once asked him.

"I don't have to," he explained. "I'm so fast I get all my work done in study hall."

Even then, Georgie was quick with his words.

Billy loved to listen to opera. Georgie heard so many while he was growing up, he thought all songs must have been written in Italian.

Georgie's interests always involved sports. In fact, they became a passion.

Years later, that passion provided LeRoy with his proudest moment. The city of Bridgewater named a baseball field in honor of his son—Sparky Anderson. On the city border, it also erected a billboard proclaiming Bridgewater as "Sparky Anderson's Home Town."

But that was many years into the future. Georgie first had a lot of growing up to do.

In 1942, the Anderson family moved to Los Angeles. Those were war years and LeRoy found work in the shipyards. With Grandpa and Grandma Anderson, the family moved into a two-bedroom house in the area which more than two decades later was the center of the Watts riot.

Georgie and Billy slept in one bedroom with their grandparents. The two younger girls slept with their parents in the other. Beverly slept on a pullout couch.

But the Andersons had made progress. There was indoor plumbing.

"I thought we had reached the promised land," Sparky now jokes. "People in California didn't have to run outside to the outhouse to use the bathroom."

The house was only two blocks from the University of Southern California baseball field. Walking past the field one day, Georgie retrieved a ball that had flown over the fence. He returned it to Coach Rod Dedeaux and a lifelong relationship began. Under Dedeaux, the USC Trojans won 11 NCAA titles to make him the winningest coach of any sport in college history.

"Georgie had a total sincerity about him," Dedeaux said. "He always stood out with his honesty. I used to give him baseballs to use on the playground when the stitches got ripped. I'd always ask him if he had helped some already loose stitches. I knew he wouldn't lie. He was reliable. And he was always so enthusiastic."

Georgie served as the USC batboy from 1943 to 1948. Not only was he exposed to the most prominent baseball coach in college history, but he also got the opportunity to work out daily with the team.

Dedeaux watched Georgie develop his skills as a ball player. He also instilled some valuable lessons that the youngster carried for life.

Dedeaux believes no job can be done without enthusiasm. If something is worth doing, then it's worth doing it with zest.

Dedeaux was a stickler for all of his players to attack the game with enthusiasm. He also wanted them to have fun along the way.

That's the way Dedeaux coached. He bubbled with enthusiasm that should have been bottled and sold to every aspiring youngster. No one worked harder. No one had more fun.

"Everybody knows how enthusiastic Tommy Lasorda is about baseball," Sparky said. "Multiply Tommy by three and you have Rod Dedeaux. If you shoved both of them into the same telephone booth, you might have a nuclear explosion. Rod taught me the value of enjoying whatever you do. Who cares what it is? Just make sure you enjoy it."

At the personal request of Georgie before he graduated, Dedeaux served as a speaker at John Adams Junior High. The principal had persuaded Georgie to invite the highly successful coach.

"The principal told me that the greatest thing that had ever happened to the school was when Georgie became batboy for USC," Dedeaux said.

"He said Georgie was always brave enough to do the right thing. He said Georgie was a natural leader and whichever way he went, the rest of the student body would follow.

"That was a tough neighborhood where he lived. A lot of the kids could have gone in the wrong direction. Georgie chose the right route and that's why the principal said he was the best thing to happen to the school. That made me feel very proud. That perfectly exemplifies Georgie Anderson."

It was the Rancho Playground, though, that provided Georgie his most enjoyable times. Rancho was a little slice of heaven that gave him everything he needed.

During the summers from dawn to dusk, Georgie and his regular group of friends lived at the playground.

"We were always there," said boyhood friend Billy Consolo. "George had to take two streetcars to get there, but he made it every day. A lot of the other kids from school would go to the beach. We played baseball. We never missed a day. We got in more swings in one day than kids nowadays get in a month."

Rancho was a mongrel mix of every ethnic persuasion. That never even occurred to any of the participants. Everyone gathered to play baseball. No one paid attention to the color of their teammates or the sounds of their last names.

"We had every ethnic group you can imagine," Consolo said. "We couldn't even pronounce all the names. Nobody cared.

"Some of the kids from 'The Little Rascals' played on our

team. The studio would drop them off in a limo and then come pick them up. They didn't get treated any differently than anyone else. The funny thing about it is our team was called the Tigers. Who would have guessed 30 years later that George and I would be part of the real Tigers?"

Because of school boundaries, Georgie was supposed to attend Polytech High. The school didn't offer baseball, however, so Georgie took two buses to attend Dorsey High where his pal Billy was enrolled.

Dorsey was a treasure chest of outstanding athletes in all sports and particularly baseball. Georgie figured that math and English had to be pretty much the same at all schools. He couldn't imagine going to one, though, that didn't offer baseball.

The baseball coach was Bud Brubaker. He was a fair but demanding coach. Once he took the field, he was all business. So were all members of the team or they weren't around for long.

Consolo played third base and Georgie played shortstop. Consolo was named Los Angeles player of the year for three straight years. After he graduated, he became one of baseball's original "bonus babies" and signed with the Boston Red Sox for a then unheard-of $75,000.

Georgie made All-City his last two years. The two were the catalysts on teams that won 42 straight games. The string still stands as a Los Angeles record.

Prior to graduation, Consolo and Anderson played on the Crenshaw Post team that captured the national American Legion championship in 1951. Also ironically, the championship game was played in Detroit's Briggs Stadium. Ten years later the park was renamed Tiger Stadium and became the site of some of Sparky's grandest professional moments.

"He had some talent," Consolo said of his lifelong friend. "He could run and had great hands. But the best thing about him was he always wanted to play. He never wanted to quit.

"He understood the game more than any of us did. He knew all the little things. He had been around older players all his life. He couldn't stand to lose. Nobody played harder.

He was a feisty little pepperpot. He never backed down from anyone and was always getting into fights. He never cared what he personally did in a game as long as his team won."

Dedeaux recognized the same qualities.

"There were some guys with much greater ability," he said. "But they played to maybe 80% of their ability. Georgie always gave you 110 %. That pushed him past guys who had more natural talent than him."

Georgie was consumed by his drive for perfection. In basketball he often was ejected from games for his overaggressive style.

"He was a good basketball player, but was always getting into trouble," Consolo laughed.

After the 11th grade, opponents didn't have to worry about Georgie on the basketball court. At that time, he dropped all outside activities to concentrate on baseball.

Lefty Phillips was a part-time scout for the Cincinnati Reds. There were plenty of players on the playground who had more talent than young George Anderson.

But Phillips appreciated Georgie's unusual drive. He had never met another kid who wanted to learn so much about baseball's little intricacies.

The two developed a special kind of kinship. Phillips convinced him to quit basketball after his junior year in order to concentrate on baseball.

"Lefty spotted something in George very early," Consolo said. "Lefty liked the way he played so hard. George looked like he knew more about the game than any of the other kids. Lefty told George's father that he reminded him of Eddie Stanky. Stanky was a big-leaguer who had the reputation of never giving up. Lefty started working with George at the playground after school every day."

By that time, George was dedicated to reaching his dream. After each session on the playground, the pair returned to the Anderson house. The two would sit on the porch for hours talking about the proper way to play the game.

Lefty had taken time to understand Georgie as a person. Although he may not have realized it when it was happening, Georgie later would appreciate how critical it is to appreciate another person's makeup.

By the time of Georgie's high school graduation, Phillips had become a full-time scout with the old Brooklyn Dodgers. One June day, Georgie graduated at noon. By one o'clock, he had signed with the Dodgers.

"I might have been able to get a few more bucks from another team," Sparky recalled. "But there was never any doubt I was gonna sign with Lefty."

The yet-to-be Sparky received $3,000 which included a salary of $250 a month for five months. Part of the deal was that he would be assigned to Santa Barbara in the California State League. That allowed LeRoy to watch his son play on weekends.

The money helped the entire Anderson household. But it really meant little to young George.

The important thing for him was that he was going to get the opportunity to play professional baseball. He had no idea what might happen once that first season was over. For him, it didn't matter. There were too many games to play before he had to think about anything like that.

Besides baseball, the only thing that captured young George Anderson's attention was Carol Valle. The two met in the fifth grade and shared the usual grammar school infatuation.

Carol thought George was "really cute." George was convinced there was not a more beautiful girl in the world.

Whatever the attraction, it obviously worked. The two have been happily married since 1953.

"They were the perfect match then and still are today," said Carol's older sister, Lovina, who with her husband Tom Sheehan, remain extremely close to the Andersons.

"He was a real clean-cut kid who cared only about sports. I've seen him mature over the years, but he's still the young boy I knew so many years ago.

"Even though he's a grandfather and might be a hero to a lot of sports fans, he hasn't changed a bit. He loves his family and he loves baseball. And he's still able to spread a little magic to everyone around him."

"AND IT DON'T COST A DIME"

Ever since I was a kid, I always had trouble with words like "there" and "their." I know "there" is someplace where I ain't. I knew how to get over there without worrying about where to put the extra "E" and forgetting about the "I." The teachers didn't like it but I always got there no matter where I was going.

Sometimes, I think, we make simple things too unsimple.

Now I wish I had a little more formal education. Thank God that I got the learning I really needed from my daddy and mama and people like Lefty Phillips.

They taught me the things that last a lifetime. They took time to give me more wisdom than I ever scraped out of a book.

Mama told me something one time early in life that I practice every day.

"We wouldn't have to spend one day in church if we treated every person we meet the way God wants us to treat everybody," she said.

Daddy wasn't religious in a formal sort of way. He just knew the difference between right and wrong. He made sure that all his kids learned that lesson before they started to mess around with spelling or trying to memorize those multiplication tables and all that other school stuff.

He said God don't know the difference in colors when

it comes to the shade of a person's skin. If He made you, then you got to be the most wonderful person in the world.

I still tell that to kids. God made you for a reason so you've got to be the most important person under the sun. God don't waste His time making jerks. We do that to ourselves.

My daddy only finished the third grade, but he was one of the wisest persons I ever knew. He also was a tough son of a gun. He told us never to go looking for a fight. If we got into one, though, he said to make that first punch count. You might not need no second.

One of the best lessons he ever taught us was the only thing in life that don't cost a dime is being nice to people. Even if you're poor, you can still be nicer than those people with all the cash.

When I look back at my childhood now, I guess we were poor. I never knew it when I was growing up, though, because we always had enough to eat and I was able to play all the baseball I ever wanted.

Being raised in the neighborhood where I grew up taught me how to fight. Not just with my fists, but with everything I had inside. It taught me how to play hard and how to treat people right.

Many years later I heard something that Woody Hayes once said. He was one of the greatest college football coaches of all time.

"If it comes easy, then it ain't worth a damn," he said.

I've always liked that quote. It's the best reason to stick to a goal that I ever heard.

Daddy never allowed no bad names or racial terms around our house. Just let one slip and he'd slap your mouth so fast your tongue played Ping-Pong with all your teeth.

I thank God every day for being raised where I was.

If it hadn't been for all that, I'm convinced I wouldn't have been so fortunate in life.

I believe the best athletes come from middle to lower class backgrounds. I ain't got nothing against the rich kids from the other side of town. But if your plate is always full, how are you gonna learn to fight to fill an empty one?

The same thing goes for the kid who wants to become a lawyer or an astronaut or anything that takes commitment. The hungry man is always going to finish on top. He's got no choice. He has to keep fighting to stay one step ahead of the wolf.

I was so lucky for all my days on the playground. We never had no new baseballs. Most of the bats we had were cracked. They were held together by nails and tape.

The umpire was always the kid on the mound. That started a lot of fights, so we learned how to negotiate in our own way. Most of the time we didn't have enough kids to make a full team. Pitcher's hands was out. So was a ball hit to right field.

None of that mattered to us. We played pickup games from sunup to sundown. Mama always knew I'd be home before it got real dark so she saved me something to eat.

It's so different today. I get more angry with the parents than I do with the kids. In fact, I think some kids get turned off to sports because of their parents.

First of all, the parents drive the kids to their games. That tells me it's the parents who want to go to the games more than the kids do. If the kids really wanted to play, they'd find their own way to the park. And they wouldn't need uniforms and umpires and scoreboards and all the other trimmings that turn the games into a big social affair.

Everything is so organized today. Too organized. How's a kid supposed to learn to swing if he's always worried about his batting average? Who cares who wins or loses as long as they play the game?

When are we gonna learn how to let them be kids? When are we gonna learn to let them have fun? We put so much pressure on our kids that by the time they turn fifteen, they're all stressed out. At thirty-five, they want another shot at becoming kids again. They missed their first time around.

Let's throw the bats and baseballs and footballs and soccer balls out on the field and let the kids pick up teams. They know how to put a game together. They might even go back to the park a little more often if they know they're going to have fun.

I guarantee you Ted Williams didn't need no fancy uniform to get in all the swings he wanted when he was a kid. I bet Michael Jordan didn't care if he was shooting baskets in a gym or some parking lot where somebody had nailed a basket to the side of a building.

I've seen parents actually screaming at their own kids for making a mistake on the field. That's laughable. Those parents ought to be videotaped and forced to watch what kind of idiots we have running around out there.

The reason for all that nonsense is money. Doesn't it always get down to dollars and cents?

When the kids are in Little League the parents want them to play good enough so they can get on the best high school teams. When they're in high school, the parents already are looking down the road for college. And if they're lucky enough to play in college, it's the parents who start looking at the pros.

We are raising our children to believe that money will solve every problem. It's an outright shame that a child don't have the chance to be a child any more.

The Little League World Series at Williamsport is a wonderful thing. Those people do a marvelous job. They even broadcast the final game over national TV.

But I'm not for it. I'm not crazy about kids becoming world champions at twelve years old. Let's give them a chance to laugh and play. Let's wait till they're at least eighteen and can make a decision on their own. Maybe by then they won't even like sports. Maybe they'll be more into science or math or something else that makes them happy.

What's wrong with that?

All the coaching in the world didn't make Johnny Bench a great baseball player or Barry Sanders a great running back. Sure, they all worked hard. But if a child grows up to be a major leaguer it's because God reached down and touched him.

I was very fortunate. I had somebody like Lefty Phillips who took an interest in me. He treated me like I was his son. He did it because I showed respect for the game. He saw me playing out there on the playground morning to night. He knew I was hungry.

What Lefty did was a lot different than most coaches, though. He didn't just teach me all the little things about baseball.

Those things are fine. But he took it one step further. He taught me the importance of setting a goal and then refusing to quit. He taught me that life ain't filled with just a bag of victories. There's a whole lot of losses that every winner has to deal with before he gets to the finish line.

Everything I ever accomplished in baseball I owe to Lefty Phillips. Without him, I would have been painting alongside of my daddy. He taught me everything I know.

Baseball ain't no different than anything else in life. Winners don't just happen. They win because they're prepared for victory—physically and mentally.

Leaving things to luck is like leaving an open can of garbage on the front porch. It's O.K. if it gets picked up. If it don't, though, things can get pretty smelly.

Lefty taught me how to prepare. He taught me how

to win. He also taught me that a loss don't have to be forever unless you let it be. A loss is only a setback. A winner is the guy who turns that setback into victory the next day.

Lefty showed all the patience in the world to a little guy who didn't have much talent. He respected my desire and for that I thank God.

I've got three World Series rings. I'm proud of each one, but I never wear them.

The reason I don't is Lefty. As far as I'm concerned, those rings belong to him. He gave me all my baseball knowledge. He taught me how to win. He warned me about all the losses that are going to jump up in everybody's life.

I gave my 1975 ring to my oldest son, Lee. My son, Albert, has the one from 1976. The 1984 ring will go to my grandson, George, when he turns eighteen. My 1970 and 1972 National League championship rings and the ones from the All-Star Games will be made into a necklace for my daughter, Shirlee.

I wouldn't trade those rings for all of Bill Gates' money. I just wouldn't feel right wearing any of them. It was Lefty who really earned them. I wish he was still around today.

Lefty never had to spend so much time on a skinny kid from the playground. He just decided to take a special interest in me.

Maybe sometimes we all ought to take a minute to thank all those teachers and people who have touched us along the way. We owe it to all of them to give a little back in return.

We may think we would have made it without them. But I guarantee you—if someone ain't there to help you when you stub your toe, you're gonna go limping for the rest of your life.

I'm not proud of some of the things I did when I played sports as a youngster. There were times when I got completely out of control. I wish somebody would have put a harness on me. I don't think I would have been a better player, but I wouldn't have been as much of a clown.

I am proud, though, that I gave everything I had every time I stepped onto a field. It didn't matter what sport. When I went into a game, the coach got everything I had to offer that day. I never took any sweat home with me. I left every drop out on that field.

That's what I tried to teach all of my players from the first day I became a manager. And that's what every parent and teacher and leader of any kind should stress to every person they may touch. If you give it everything you've got, let somebody else worry about what happens.

I was very lucky. I got all this from my parents and people like Lefty. They deserve the credit. They took the time to help a kid who could not have made it all alone.

It's All About People

Throughout Sparky's career, he was often compared to the legendary Casey Stengel.

If "The Old Professor" were alive today, he would welcome the comparison to Sparky Anderson. More than anyone else, Casey could truly appreciate Sparky's singular charm.

No manager in history ever challenged Casey's stranglehold on championships. From 1949 through 1960, Casey managed those storybook Yankee teams that produced ten American League pennants and seven World Series championships. They featured magical names like Mickey Mantle and Yogi Berra and Roger Maris and Whitey Ford.

Although they didn't grab as many gold trophies, Sparky's Cincinnati Reds arguably came closest to matching the Yankees for sheer on-field dominance for a shorter period of time.

Those teams were loaded with their own roster of magical names—Johnny Bench and Joe Morgan and Pete Rose and Tony Perez.

There are other more striking similarities between Casey and the equally loquacious Sparky.

The legend of Casey was carved by far more than sheer baseball brilliance. His peculiar quirks and bent for showmanship transformed him into a legitimate American folk hero.

He fractured the English language like a runaway jackhammer on a pile of brittle bricks. He jumbled words and twisted phrases. Mesmerized listeners chuckled. They simply felt good listening to the "old man" spin countless stories about baseball and life according to Casey.

"When I was a kid, Casey used to work us out at the playground during the off-season," said Rod Dedeaux who coached the University of Southern California to 11 NCAA titles. He also took the young Georgie Anderson under his wing when Georgie was only nine. "Casey talked baseball till it got dark. He lectured us like he was Socrates."

Sparky perfected his own style of storytelling. Sometimes it takes two left turns and three loops to the right. English teachers might shudder at his grammar . . . or lack of it.

Some of his words can't be found in a dictionary. That's because some of his words, in the true sense, aren't really words at all.

Somehow, though, Sparky always makes his point. And there are usually a few chuckles along the way.

"Casey and Georgie are out of the same mold," Dedeaux said. "They both loved people so much. By their personality and presentation, they were able to sell their ideas. They always had a way of putting on a show. They're the same in all ways and every one is complimentary. And that includes the results."

No managers in history appreciated the baseball stage as much as Casey and Sparky. They loved an audience and lived to perform. For them, baseball was meant to be fun. And it was their jobs to make everybody laugh along with them.

Above all else, both shared a passion for people. Nothing meant more than making people feel good.

For years, Sparky has touted Tommy Lasorda as baseball's best ambassador. Lasorda is flattered, but concedes the unofficial crown to Sparky.

"You have to remember, Sparky operated out of a couple of cities like Cincinnati and Detroit that aren't giant media markets," Lasorda said. "But because of his personality, enthusiasm, and true love for the game, he gave a boost to baseball that nobody else could have done.

"There's a lot of Casey in Sparky. He genuinely loves people. That's no act that Sparky puts on. He treats everybody the same way he treats his own family."

Just as Casey did, Sparky has always had trouble differentiating between people simply according to position or supposed social status.

As Sparky innocently explains: "People is people and there ain't no kinda people better than nobody else."

It's this innocence that makes Sparky feel as comfortable with the bellhop as he is with the president of a luxury hotel.

During his last several seasons as manager of the Tigers, Sparky used to bring George McCarthy to spring training. Sparky never allowed McCarthy to see a bill. Sparky covered the six-week tab and even shared his hotel room with "the old man."

McCarthy is a ninety-something retired "ambassador of life." He raised a beautiful family, has more grandchildren than he can count and thoroughly enjoyed squeezing out a living from hundreds of jobs he picked up along the way. The one he loved most was caretaker of the animals that were used for scientific experiments at Yale University.

"I learned a little something about life from every job I ever had," McCarthy says proudly. "So at least I know a hundred things."

McCarthy is short enough to look up to a jockey. He's skinny enough to have to run around the shower to get wet. The beak he calls his nose easily keeps his lips from getting sun-burned. The gravel in his voice is a grindstone to sharpen his caustic wit.

If a movie were to be shot on the life of George Burns, all McCarthy would need is a toupee, a cigar, and a leading lady to play Gracie Allen. No one could tell the difference.

Don't worry about the jokes. McCarthy would provide his own material.

If a man is truly judged by the company he keeps, George McCarthy makes Sparky a king.

Neither Sparky nor McCarthy is exactly sure when or even how they met. Somehow one day, both felt they had known each other for all of their lives.

Each one whispers a silent prayer of thanks to God for their rich friendship. Of course, neither will admit it and would adamantly deny it if one even suspected the other.

"Why in the hell he ever picked me, I don't know," Mc-

Carthy said. "I'm just a nobody, but that's the kind of guy he is. If he likes you, he likes you. It doesn't matter what you do for a living.

"He needs me like he needed some pitcher on the disabled list. But he always treats me the same way he treats all of those Hall of Fame guys he knows. Here I was an old man and he used to take me down to Florida and treat me like a prince. He's the kind of guy who leaves footprints on your heart."

Because of his stature in baseball and his naturally magnetic personality, Sparky's spectrum of acquaintances ranges from Presidents of the United States to peanut vendors in the ballparks.

Over the years, Sparky was privileged to have met Presidents Nixon, Ford, and Bush. He also has met a cast of celebrated characters from the worlds of entertainment, politics, and business.

He's as comfortable swapping stories with such celebrities as he is with the cab driver who merely wants to know why he made a certain pitching change in the eighth inning of last night's game.

"That's a unique capability and there's no question Sparky has it," said Former President Gerald R. Ford, the nation's 38th president. "He was comfortable with people like myself and Nixon and Bush and they were comfortable with him."

Mr. Ford remains impressed with Sparky's ability to float gracefully between a maze of widely differing personalities.

"You could see it on the ball field when he was with the Cincinnati Reds and Detroit Tigers," Mr. Ford continued. "Both of those teams had a broad spectrum of personalities and Sparky had a good rapport with all of them."

Mr. Ford served as President during the period of Cincinnati's back-to-back world championship years of 1975–76.

"Before I met Sparky I was an admirer of his," Mr. Ford said. "When you heard his name and saw what he did with the Reds and the Tigers, it really generated interest and enthusiasm. When you associate that name 'Sparky' with his style of management, it just tells you that here's a fellow who gets the best out of his ball team."

After meeting Sparky for the first time, Mr. Ford was satisfied that the man lived up to the reputation that had preceded him. He was bubbly, intense, enthusiastic, and always in control.

"He's the guy that you envision," Mr. Ford said. "You get exactly what you expect. You anticipate someone who has a lot of zest and enthusiasm. He has his own way of speaking, but it's totally acceptable. It's his personality."

At a recent meeting in Grand Rapids, Michigan, Mr. Ford still was impressed with Sparky's enthusiasm.

"He'll always remain the same," Mr. Ford said. "I'm very proud of our friendship. Because we're both interested in athletics, competition, and young people, we share a lot of rapport."

Sparky has never been one to seek friendships based strictly on social or political status. Because of his engaging personality, however, many socially and politically powerful acquaintances have been established. When forced to make a preference, however, Sparky somehow always chooses the man who carries his lunch bucket to work.

"I remember walking through downtown Cincinnati with him when I was a little girl," recalled Sparky's daughter Shirlee. "We'd see homeless people. They just wanted to shake his hand. He'd always stop and talk with them. Then when he got to the park, he might talk to the President.

"He always had time to give a genuine smile. He may not use proper English, but it doesn't matter. There's too much judgment and thinking about what a person does in his life. That never has mattered to my father. His job just happened to put him in the limelight. If everybody was like him, we'd all get along."

James Blanchard served as Democratic Governor of Michigan from 1983 through 1990 and appreciated what Sparky's reputation meant for his state. He later served as United States Ambassador to Canada and discovered the international extent of Sparky's celebrity.

"When I was in Canada, I saw how world-renowned

Sparky really is," Blanchard said. "When people discovered I was from Michigan, before we conducted any business they'd all ask, 'Do you know Sparky?'

"Sparky is one of those true baseball characters that is clearly one of the most respected figures in North America. He didn't earn that reputation just from what he did on the diamond. It also comes from the type of human being he is."

Sparky had been the Tiger manager for three and a half years when Blanchard first took office in Michigan. Upon meeting the new young governor for the first time, Sparky told Blanchard's aide to select six dates at which he would appear to help the youth in the state.

"He's a role model," Blanchard said. "A first-rate role model. He helped to promote our youth corps and helped in our anti-drug campaign. He was always involved in a variety of charity work and never charged a dime."

Sparky enjoys himself with whomever he's around. His sense of humor runs on cruise control. He treats any state governor the same way he treats the man who delivers his mail.

"On a variety of occasions, Sparky let me know that he was of the Republican persuasion," Blanchard joked. "But he never let that interfere with our friendship."

That differing political persuasion, in fact, is the source of one of Blanchard's most cherished memories.

"There was a year I visited Sparky in spring training," Blanchard said. "The Tigers were playing a game against Boston in Winter Haven. Sparky spotted Ted Williams and took me over to meet him. He told Williams, 'Aw, Ted, you gotta meet this guy. He's our governor and he's great.'

"We were posing for a picture when Williams said to Sparky, 'He is an R (Republican) isn't he?' Sparky said, 'No, Ted, but he's still all right.' Williams crushed me with a hug and bellowed, 'You're a D (Democrat)?' That picture means the world to me. I truly miss seeing Sparky around."

Bo Schembechler became acquainted with Sparky shortly after he was named manager of the Detroit Tigers in 1979. After Schembechler became president of the Tigers in 1990, he came to understand the essence of his manager.

"There's no great secret why he's accomplished so much," Schembechler said. "He loves people. That says it all. He treats the lowest person on the staff as if that person was president of the company."

Schembechler was particularly impressed with Sparky's ability to learn about everyone around him.

"He knew the names of everybody on the staff," Schembechler said. "I'm not talking about just the players. I'm talking about all the front office staff and everyone who worked inside that stadium. He took time to say hello to everyone and call them by name. He even knew a little bit about most of their families."

Schembechler also appreciates the time Sparky extended to him.

"Whenever I had a question about baseball, he gave me an answer that explained the situation right down to the bone," Schembechler said. "Some of the questions might have seemed dumb to somebody who had been in baseball his whole life. That didn't matter to Sparky. All he needed to know was that you were interested and he'd answer everything. And he wasn't afraid to give an opinion."

Schembechler has influenced countless thousands of lives during his college coaching career. He has the wisdom to appreciate a true leader.

"I don't care about any of his numbers in the record books," Schembechler said. "Sparky should be judged on what he does for other people. Children. Adults. All those nondescript people who may not mean much to anyone else. That's the kind of person he is. He just happened to be a helluva good baseball manager."

Schembechler is convinced Sparky's ability to deal with every type of individual was the real secret to his professional success.

"I don't think any manager can make a great team out of an average one or an average team out of a bad one," Schembechler said. "I do think if Sparky Anderson has the talent, he will win. He will flat out win every time.

"Even when he had a team without much talent, that team played hard. There was harmony in the clubhouse.

There was never any bitching or crying. That's the sign of a great manager."

Even Sparky was moved by one of his brief encounters with whom he calls the "ultimate celebrity." The meeting occurred in 1988 in Hamtramck, Michigan. It's a blue-collar town surrounded by the city of Detroit on all four borders.

Pope John Paul II appeared in Hamtramck during his visit to the United States. Through his friendship with Detroit's Cardinal Edmund Szoka, Sparky was privileged to shake the Pontiff's hand. He received a personal blessing as thousands of Detroiters cheered.

"This is one person who is different from the rest of us," Sparky said. "He took my hand and said 'Bless you, my son.' And I'll guarantee you he never heard of nobody named Sparky."

Even to this day, Sparky tingles at the memory.

"Some people you meet have a lot of glitter and all that stuff," Sparky said. "This was something totally different.

"I'll never forget the Pope's face. When you looked into his eyes, you could tell he cared about every living person in the world. He don't care about a person's religion. He don't care what anybody does for a living. But he cares about every person because he knows we are all children of God. He's the greatest person I ever had the privilege to meet."

In 1994 in honor of his sixtieth birthday, Sparky received an unexpected surprise. Through the efforts of Lakeland, Florida Bishop Norbert Dorsey, Sparky received a baseball signed "With blessing" by Pope John Paul II.

The Pope has blessed people all over the world. Probably never before, though, has he been asked to sign a baseball.

"I never collected no autographs and never understood why people get so excited over them," Sparky said, "but I'll always treasure this. The Pope is the symbol of everything good in the world. This baseball will stay in the Anderson family forever."

Sparky's friendship with President Nixon spanned several years. Sparky was always amazed at the President's insight into baseball and his ability to act like "one of the boys."

"He used to ask me that if defense means so much to a good team, then why don't the papers run the leading defensive players like they do for the hitters and pitchers," Sparky said. "The man had a point."

But it's the everyday people with whom Sparky has always felt most comfortable.

"Sparky's the kind of guy who can have his shoes shined in the airport and wind up taking the shoe shine man to dinner that night," Schembechler said. "And the next morning Sparky might be on the phone with the President."

The way Sparky has it figured, the man shining those shoes has as much class as anybody wearing them.

About the Real People

I know God has a sense of humor. If He didn't, I never wouldda been hooked up with George McCarthy.

Georgie is the all-time character I ever met in my life. He looks more like George Burns than George Burns did when he was alive. I think he's older than Burns was and I ain't too sure that he ain't even funnier.

Neither one of us are exactly sure how it happened, but we started to pal around about 20 years ago. I can honestly say Georgie's been my gift from God.

If you name any kind of job, Georgie's done it. He's a little bit of con man and a little bit of a priest. For all anybody knows, at one time or another, he might have been both.

When we get to talking, sometimes I ask him if there's anything he hasn't done. And what does it matter anyway?

Georgie never had to impress anybody. He knew who he was.

He never had no money, but he raised a beautiful family. He found out early in life that he was always the happiest when he had to hustle for his next dollar.

He has this marvelous way of appreciating everything that life has given him. He stays so sharp because he keeps himself involved with everything he can put his hands on.

When I took him to spring training, I used to joke with him all the time.

"Just don't die down here," I told him. "It's too much trouble to get your body back to California and I've got a baseball team to run."

He got the biggest kick out of meeting all the players and giving baseballs to the little kids at the park. That's when he was happiest. I could see it in his eyes. In his own little way, he was making someone else feel good.

Georgie originally came from the East Coast. I thought he really would die the day we played the Boston Red Sox and I introduced him to Ted Williams. Even Williams got a kick out of joking with the "old man."

I truly appreciated being able to take him to spring training. It had nothing to do with the position I held and the fact that he was retired. This was not a case of charity. It was a relationship that worked both ways.

In fact, if anybody got the best of the deal it was me. I learned so much from Georgie. As far as understanding people, I think I've learned as much from him as I did from my mother and father.

Georgie taught me never to be dazzled by the color of a silk necktie. He said the grease stains on a man's hands are worth a whole lot more than a fancy pair of new shoes.

I've been very fortunate in my life. I've met a lot of people who we like to call celebrities. I'm thankful for those opportunities. But I think when we start to measure people, we ought to look at somebody like George McCarthy.

People like Georgie are precious. They ain't smiles for dollars. There ain't nothing hiding up under their sleeves except maybe some grease stains from years of hard work.

There are plenty of Georgies in every city. Some are teachers in the classrooms where your kids go to school. Some work in the bakery shop down the street.

They're everyday people who care about their friends

and families. They don't give a damn if their neighbor makes a few bucks more than they do. They're happy with themselves.

Georgie reminds me a little bit about Casey Stengel. All of Casey's records speak for themselves.

Forget about those records when you talk about Casey. He could have been an actor. He could have been in the circus. He hypnotized people with the way he talked. He was always on stage. And he was always promoting baseball.

I've heard all the comparisons about Casey and me. Believe me, I'm honored. But it ain't fair to compare Casey with anybody. He was almost from another planet. The rest of us are digging out from a molehill compared to the "old man."

What really knocks me out was the way Casey treated people. The guy at the corner newsstand got as much of his attention as the bank president. Sometimes more, if the guy on the corner started to talk about baseball.

The great thing about Casey was that he knew how to love Casey first. He accepted himself and loved himself. That allowed him to love everybody else. I've always said that if you love yourself first more than anything, then you will throw that love off to everyone you meet.

How in the hell is anybody supposed to love you if you don't care enough about yourself to do it first?

Casey knew who he was. He knew he had a special calling. He knew people loved to be around him. And he never failed to give them a show.

Anybody who ever had the chance to meet him is still talking about that time today. That's a special gift when people remember the day they met you.

I was so lucky to be with Casey on a number of occasions. After he found out Carol and I got married when we were nineteen, he nicknamed me "Shotgun." He said her father must have come after me loaded with buckshot.

The only thing I will admit to sharing with Casey is a genuine love for people. I don't care if it's a cop, a con man, a priest or a bookie, you can find something good in just about everybody.

If we just take the time to treat people the way we want to be treated, we generally find most of them are just like us.

One time after I started managing the Reds, my daddy asked me how I handled being around all those "big" people.

I looked at Daddy and told him—when you get up in the morning, you gotta put on your pants, put on your shirt, put on your socks and put on your shoes. Then you go to work every day.

All them "big" people gotta do the same thing. But you raised five children working hard and working honest. Some of those "big" people never had to do it the hard way. So far, I ain't met any one to your equal.

And to this day, I still haven't.

What difference does it make what a person does to earn a living as long as he's honest and does the best job he can every day?

What makes a ball player better than a mailman? What makes the manager of a baseball team better than a manager in a supermarket? Or even the boy bagging the groceries if he's packing those bags the best that he can?

A player and a manager might make more money. But they ain't better than those other guys if those other guys are doing the best job they can.

Just because a person is on television all the time, does that make him a big shot? I always figure a waitress in a restaurant could be my mother or sister. The guy flipping hamburgers could be my father or brother. So I better treat everybody with the respect I want my family to receive.

For a lot of years when I managed in Detroit, Carol

worked as a salesperson in the drugstore up the street from our house.

Nobody knew her husband was Sparky. Even if they did, nobody cared. Carol worked there because she liked it. And she did the best job she could every day she went in.

We can classify jobs. We can't classify people. Not as long as those people are doing those jobs as honestly and the best they can.

What does it hurt to say "hello" or "thank you" to people? If those are bad words, let's rip them out of the dictionary right now.

I remember one of the first road trips we took after I joined the Tigers. We were riding on the team bus when one of the players yelled, "Hey, bussee . . . give us some air."

I stood up and walked down the aisle. Suddenly the bus got as quiet as a funeral home when I stood in front of the player who had shouted.

"Young man," I growled at him so that there was no mistaking I was more serious than the Pope.

"This bus driver's name happens to be Herman. And if you had taken the time to look at the nameplate right in front of you, you would have known that, without me having to tell you. Now if you ask Herman politely, maybe he'll listen. But until you do, maybe Herman will just keep on driving and pretend you're not even here."

Herman had the right to be treated with respect like everybody else. Maybe it's just a little thing. But if we put all those little things together, we just might wind up with something good.

We must remember that the most important person in the world is the one standing next to us when we go to the market tomorrow.

It ain't so bad to slip him a smile. You might just find out you'll get one in return.

If at First You Don't Succeed . . .

Sparky's professional playing career was inversely proportional to his colorful managerial legend.

It was gloriously mediocre.

Sparky made it to the major leagues for one season in 1959. That was with the Philadelphia Phillies, so he must have felt right at home.

The Phillies were awful. Most of the time, they played like a minor league team. About the best thing the Phillies did that year was finish the season. They didn't forfeit any games and they showed up on time for all of them. They wound up losing 90 of their 154 games.

Nevertheless, Sparky played in all but two games. He batted .218 with no home runs and 34 runs batted in. He quickly jokes that with any luck, though, he could have hit .225. A couple of times during batting practice, he hit one off the wall.

After the season, he was back in the minors where it looked like he was destined to spend the rest of his career.

He spent 16 years in the minor leagues as a player or manager. If nothing else, the tedious apprenticeship proved Sparky's persistence surpassed his humble playing abilities.

Sparky is living proof that if someone wants something bad enough in life, he can't be afraid to give some sweat . . . and maybe even bleed.

"Sparky was always the underdog," Kirk Gibson said. "He was a little guy with a huge desire in his heart. He beat the odds. Nobody knew who the hell George Anderson was. And who was this Sparky guy? After he started to win, people began to listen. He ignored what he was not supposedly able to do.

"People have a way of labeling people as failures for one reason or another. People underestimated what Sparky's really made of. Sparky has a big heart. He willed his way to the top. People who are afraid to gut it out in life ought to take a look at the little man."

Throughout his professional playing career, Sparky never hit .300. His tops for home runs was five in a year—all in the minor leagues.

"He wasn't the type of player that would dazzle you," said George Scherger who was Sparky's first professional manager at Santa Barbara in 1953. He later became one of Sparky's coaches at Cincinnati.

"He was more of a manager's player," Scherger continued. "He was a real feisty guy. Nothing scared him. All he wanted to do was win. I knew there was something special about him because he never wanted to leave the field."

Sparky was always wise enough to realize his true ticket to the pros. His talent was short, so he had to play harder than the next guy.

In his first spring training at the Dodgers' Vero Beach, Florida camp, there were 26 minor league teams. That meant there was a total of 512 players all fighting for jobs.

On the pecking order of pure talent, Sparky figured maybe 510 were better than he was.

"Ray Charles could have looked at those guys and seen they were better than me," Sparky admitted. "I just knew I could do other things better than most of them. Whatever they taught me, I picked up fast. Nobody had to tell me nothing twice. Lefty Phillips had taught me well. I could absorb things easy because I was prepared. Baseball was easy for me to absorb. And I promised myself that no human being would work harder."

Sparky spent seven years in the International League in which Toronto had a team. After each season, the *Toronto Globe & Mail* published a poll rating the league's top players in a variety of categories. For all seven years Sparky was voted "smartest player in the league."

"They weren't talking about books either," Sparky cracked.

All the hard work kept him in the pros. Except for his one year with Philadelphia, however, he couldn't make it to the big leagues.

"He was small and his size was against him," said Harry Schwegman who was a roommate of Sparky's for three minor league seasons.

"But he was so dedicated to the game. When he wasn't playing, all he wanted to do was talk baseball. He never drank alcohol. After games, we'd sit around for hours. He'd be drinking a soda talking and talking baseball. I never dreamed he would go on to manage like he did, but I knew he'd stay in baseball. He was that determined."

Managing never was Sparky's long-range goal, even though one year in spring training the former Dodger player boss, Al Campanis, told a group of writers, "that Anderson kid is going to manage in the big leagues one day."

While playing for Charlie Dressen at Toronto in 1962, Sparky got another break. Dressen managed in the major leagues for 16 seasons and appeared in two World Series with the Dodgers.

"You're going to manage some day," Dressen told Sparky. "So from now on, if you've got any questions about what's going on in the game, you come and ask me."

Dressen had a reputation for being one of the finest handlers of pitchers in the game. Sparky never wasted an opportunity to learn more about baseball.

"Charlie wasn't the best manager I ever played for," Sparky said. "But he knew more about pitching than any other one I played for. I took a lot from him."

Scherger recognized the Dressen pitching influence on Sparky.

"Sparky was uncanny when it came to handling pitchers," Scherger said. "When we were at Cincinnati, he got to be known as 'Captain Hook' because of the way he used to replace his pitchers all the time.

"He knew what he was doing. He studied pitchers. Once a game started, he never took his eyes off them. He had a feel for when a pitcher was running out of gas. He always made sure he made a move before something bad happened. Even if a move backfired, he figured it was better to get burned by doing something than sitting around and doing nothing at all."

If Sparky wasn't the model student in school, he never missed a lesson after he started to work. He never blew the opportunity to learn everything he could from everyone around him. He studied each manager, coach, and instructor he encountered. He stole their strongest traits. He tried to eliminate their shortcomings.

"The three smartest guys I ever seen in the game were George Scherger, George Kissel and Clay Bryant," Sparky said.

From Scherger, Sparky learned the importance of preparation and intensity.

"Nobody's better on fundamentals than Scherger," he said. "And nobody got into a game more than him. He managed every game like it was the seventh game of the World Series. Me and him were getting kicked out of games all the time."

From Kissel, Sparky learned that as in life, attention to even the smallest detail can make the difference between success and failure.

"For every phase of the game, Kissel is the best there ever was," Sparky said. "He told me baseball ain't no different than any other profession. The guy who pays attention to all the little things is gonna finish ahead of the guy who's sloppy. The sloppy guy just lets things slip away. The guy who pays attention to details is two steps ahead of everybody else.

"Base stealing, for instance, ain't done on speed alone. Knowing a pitcher's move and getting the right leadoff puts an extra step even on a mule. Kissel's been in the St. Louis organization since before they brewed Budweiser there. Nobody can touch him for details."

From Bryant, Sparky learned that until someone learns to respect a loss, it's impossible to appreciate the meaning of victory.

"A loss is supposed to hurt," Sparky said. "If you never broke a finger you don't know what it means to play over pain. Winners get hurt. They just know how to deal with it.

"I played two years for Bryant. He was the toughest S.O.B. you ever met. He never let us forget what we learned from a loss. We learned to respect it. We learned it's only a setback that can be used for victory."

Sparky's lengthy but undistinguished playing career ended in 1964. At thirty years old, he was named manager of Toronto in the International League by owner Jack Kent Cooke. The wealthy businessman, who went on to own the Washington Redskins of the National Football League, had likened Sparky to former major league manager Alvin Dark. Dark had always been considered to be one of baseball's shrewdest managers.

Sparky was impressed by the compliment. He quickly responded by telling the media that "if I can't win with this club, I ought to be fired."

Toronto finished fifth. And Sparky got his pink slip.

That was only one of the young manager's mistakes on his trip to major league legend. The fiery spirit that punctuated his playing career only got hotter when he took over the reins. The connotation of the name "Sparky" became more appropriate with each passing season.

Sparky's ejection from a game became a somewhat regular feature. His wife told him she always made sure to show up before the first inning. She was never sure how long he would stay in a game. His post-game tantrums after a loss sometimes looked like big-time wrestling.

Once he splattered watermelon over the clubhouse walls and ceiling. Squished food and locker stools went flying like missiles. After one particularly frustrating loss, Sparky had to be restrained from firing a portable television set further than one of his infielders could toss a ball.

The ultimate outburst that almost wrote Sparky's ticket out of the game, but at least helped to harness his misguided enthusiasm, occurred in 1965 when he managed at Rock Hill, South Carolina.

In one of the most heated arguments of his career,

Sparky tried to make his point by grabbing an umpire by the throat. After the hurricane subsided and Sparky was in the locker room, he began packing his belongings for what he thought was the last time.

"I honestly thought my career was over," he said. "I don't care how mad you get, you don't go around grabbing anybody by the throat. I thought for sure I was gonna get banned for life."

Before Sparky had his bags packed, the umpire entered the clubhouse through the back door.

"You know something," he told a startled Sparky. "I bumped you first. I apologize for that. Why don't we forget what happened and let's go from there."

Sparky told him he'd never forget him. He also learned to keep his hands in his back pockets when arguing an umpire's call. There would be no second chance. He never thought he'd get a first one.

"There might have been times when Sparky got out of control," said Tommy Lasorda who spent two years as Sparky's teammate in the minor leagues.

"I know he never meant any harm and I'm sure he's sorry for those occasions. He just had such great desire. He was so competitive. He played by all the rules, but he'd do anything to win. Nothing meant anything to Sparky except for winning. That's the way he came up as a player and that's the way he managed throughout his career."

Sparky's minor league paycheck didn't come close to supporting a growing family. Each year when the season ended, he was out on the street looking for another job.

"One thing I never did was collect unemployment," Sparky says proudly. "I refused to do it."

The jobs were a potpourri of blue collar America.

He worked as a pipe cutter in an antenna manufacturing plant; he stocked and unloaded boxes at Sears & Roebuck; he ran a drill press; he worked in a doughnut shop.

"That was a great job, but I got too heavy from eating all my products," he cracked.

The closest he came to white collar work were a couple of off-season stints as an automobile salesman. Neither one was successful because Sparky refused to sell a vehicle to young people who really couldn't afford the payments.

"I'd look at their credit statement and tell them they couldn't afford a new car," he said. "I'd tell them to invest some money in their old car and drive it till it died."

"You know they're gonna buy a new car from someone else," his sales manager argued.

"Yeah . . . but not from me," Sparky replied.

If honesty meant anything, Sparky figured the couple would return at the proper time.

While a player and later as a minor league manager, Sparky spent a few winters participating in the Latin American leagues for extra money.

After he managed the Asheville, South Carolina minor league team to a pennant in the 1968 season, he was asked by new San Diego Padres Manager Preston Gomez to serve as one of his coaches. Sparky was back in the major leagues. Little did he know that this time it was for the rest of his career.

He never expected what waited for him the following season. No one could have guessed that he would be in the dugout of the Cincinnati Reds as head of the team that evolved into The Big Red Machine.

Sometimes persistence has a strange way of paying dividends. If someone is unafraid to knock on enough doors, eventually one of them is going to open.

Sparky displayed nothing but persistence in various big cities and even more little towns speckled across North America during his minor league career. There was Santa Barbara . . . Pueblo . . . Fort Worth . . . Montreal . . . Toronto . . . Rock Hill . . . St. Petersburg . . . Modesto . . . Asheville.

Eventually his show would play in the big cities of the National League and over television screens across the country.

Before long, every baseball fan would become familiar with the character named Sparky.

Learning from the Bottom Up

I was only thirty-five years old when I went to my first spring training as manager of the Cincinnati Reds. I had spent a whole career in the minor leagues. The big boys call them the "bushes" because most of the clubs are somewhere out in the country away from the big cities.

There were some big-time big boys on that Cincinnati team who already had paid their dues.

Pete Rose had seven seasons under his belt and was coming off back-to-back batting championships. Tony Perez had been there six years and had established himself as a legitimate power hitter.

Johnny Bench only had me beat by three years. But all the experts already were calling him the greatest catcher to come along since they started to put padding in the catcher's mitt.

That team was like a giant balloon. It was pumped full of pure oil. And it was getting ready to explode into The Big Red Machine. It was the best team of the '70s anywhere on the planet.

It didn't take long for those guys to label me the "minor leaguer."

I'll never forget the first meeting I had with them.

"Gentlemen, let me tell you something," I started. "I came from the minor leagues which I loved very much. And don't think for a minute I'll ever be scared to go back because this don't mean a thing to me. The minor leagues, gentlemen, is what I truly love."

They thought I was crazy. Maybe I could handle going back to the minors, but none of them had any intention of leaving Cincinnati.

Of course, I didn't want to leave either. I spent 16 years bouncing around little towns all over the country and South America. That's a lot of bus rides and way too many greasy hamburgers in the middle of the night.

The funny thing about it is that I'm glad I had served my time. It's just like the kid who goes away to college. Those whole four years he wishes he was out in the real world making a living. When he looks back, though, he realizes he had spent some of the best years of his life in school.

I was lucky. I didn't waste a day in the minors wishing all the time that I'd get a call to the big leagues. I enjoyed every minute because I was doing something I loved.

Sometimes I wish people would just slow down a bit to appreciate the things they've got. They might find out what they're wishing for ain't as good as whatever they've got.

A lot of people—even a lot of people in baseball—don't know that the minor leagues is where all the fun is.

I took it to extremes and thought I'd always be in baseball. I never thought anything bad could happen.

That's the scary part I want all young people to understand. It's all right to chase a dream. But don't stand there naked and let that dream turn into a nightmare. Prepare yourself for when some kind of dog jumps up and bites you when you ain't looking. That ain't giving up. That's staying a step ahead of the dog.

I thought everything was always gonna be the same. I'd play ball and the game would never end. That ninth inning always comes around, though. I was lucky. Even when I think about it today, I still get the shivers.

Sure, I wanted to make it to the bigs. But even if I had stayed in the minor leagues my whole life, I wouldda been happy.

The players call the major leagues "showtime." For me, I enjoyed the show in the minor leagues.

I loved it there. I guess everybody thinks about getting to the majors some day. But as long as I was playing, I really didn't care where it was.

All of us can't be the president of a company. If everyone was a general, there'd be no soldiers in the army. But every one of us can take pride in the job that we do. It might not be the most glamorous one, but we all have the chance to be the best at whatever it is.

Wherever I was playing, that was the big leagues to me. What the hell did I know about Brooklyn when I was playing at Santa Barbara? Except for what I saw in my old geography book, I never really knew for sure that Brooklyn actually existed.

I never looked in the papers to see who was winning in the big leagues. When I was at Santa Barbara, all I cared about was what was going on in the California State League. When I went to Fort Worth, I cared about the Texas League. And when I got to Montreal, all I worried about was the International League.

As long as I could play, all the other guys could do all the worrying they wanted.

From a pure coaching perspective, managing in the minor leagues is much more rewarding than in the majors. All those kids there paid attention. They were too afraid to do anything else. I remember back to grade school and I got scared when a teacher walked into the room. By the time I was a senior, I thought I knew more than the whole staff.

When you're running a minor league club, there ain't no other coaches. It's all you, so you better know what you're doing. And you better love every minute because in that job you ain't punching a time clock.

There ain't no writers around asking why you made this move or why you didn't make that one. There's no television cameras that take you away from your work. You might only have a couple hundred people in the stands because half the town might not even know there's a minor league team there. But who cares?

There ain't no glitz and glitter. It's the pure package without all the fancy trimmings.

In the major leagues, the boys are in it for the gold. They drive up to the park in their Mercedes and Jaguars. The big four-wheelers got to be the fad for a while. Next year there'll probably be a new one. Maybe it'll be those Brinks trucks for when they pick up their paychecks.

In the minor leagues, you might have three or four guys driving to the park together in a beat-up junker. They're all hungry because they're fighting to get to the bigs. Some of a player's longest-lasting friendships begin in the minor leagues.

I never really thought about it till Bo Schembechler came to the Tigers. He asked me why they called us managers in baseball instead of coaches. Weren't we supposed to be coaching these young men? A manager sounds like you're running a gas station or a supermarket.

The more I thought about it, the more it made sense.

Think about all the great names in coaching and then you understand what Bo was talking about. There's Bo . . . Bobby Knight . . . Dean Smith . . . John Wooden . . . Rod Dedeaux . . . Woody Hayes . . . Bear Bryant and a whole lot more.

They had a set of rules. And those rules were there for Freddy. They were there for Johnny. They were there for Jimmy. And they were there for Bobby. The rules were the rules and they didn't have no names attached to them. If somebody broke them, they were punished just like everybody else.

Everybody knew the rules coming in. When they recruited a young man, his parents knew exactly what to expect. Those parents could sleep at night because they knew their boys were in good hands.

When those four years were over, they knew their boy was gonna walk out of that school a man.

Schembechler and Knight and all those other great coaches didn't zigzag down the highway. There might be some bumps in the road, but they didn't make no bad turns. They ran straight down the middle and expected everybody with them to run the same route.

That's discipline. That's organization. That's learning to live within a system and making a contribution for the good of the team.

That don't apply just to sports. Any successful operation is based on the same principles. And there ain't nothing better a young man or woman can develop in life than discipline.

A disciplined person with a little talent will reach more goals than a sloppy person with a lot more talent.

Most people have a misconception about the big leagues. The big leagues have an awful lot of good managers. But don't think the minor leagues or the colleges don't have coaches that are just as good, if not better.

Bo and Knight and Smith and a lot of the great ones could have gone into the pros. They could have set records there.

The reason they stayed at the college level is because they enjoy coaching so much. When you coach in college or manage in the minor leagues you actually get the opportunity to help shape a boy into a man, or a man into a leader. If you stay there for five, seven, or ten years, you actually see the same person coming through all the time. He's in a different body and he might come from a different part of the country, but it's basically the same kid. Now it's your job to help him develop.

I think that's one of the real rewards that parents and teachers share. The opportunity to influence the lives of our youngsters is more of a gift to the adults than it is to the kids.

The real good coaches and managers learn from their players. They help to shape the youngsters. In the process, they learn how to become better teachers themselves.

That's why I was so fortunate to have signed with the Dodgers when I got out of school.

If you were a Dodger, it didn't matter at what level you played. You were a Dodger the same as Sandy Koufax or Roy Campanella or Jackie Robinson.

The difference between the Dodgers and so many other organizations is that they had a program that started at the top and continued the same way all the way down to their lowest team of their minor league system. Everything was done the same way. There was discipline.

It was the same way with the Reds under Bob Howsam. No minor league kid was gonna tear up a hotel room or a clubhouse. If he acted like an idiot, then he was going to pay the price. That's discipline.

If a young player was willing to pay attention and take advantage of those programs, he was going to get the most out of his God-given talent.

It's the same for kids who ain't into sports. They have gifts but they can't take them for granted. A student don't become a scholar just by carrying books home from school. It takes work. It takes discipline.

Who can't remember teachers saying, "You'll be sorry one day that you didn't study harder in school."

Every one of those teachers was right. I was one of those kids who laughed. It still comes back to bite me in a lot of little different ways.

Everybody gets one chance. The trick is not to blow it.

School is a lot like the minor leagues. If you really learn to appreciate the discipline, you'll be ready for all those big games you'll have to face in life.

The Big Red Machine

Finally those all-night bus rides came to an end for Sparky.

He still was gone all summer long. Now, however, the trips were made on jet planes. The roadside inns now became first class downtown hotels.

Sparky's menu has always been basic burger. At least now, though, meal money covered more than those grease patties from the all-night "Burger and Burp."

Sparky made it to the major leagues as a coach under manager Preston Gomez for the San Diego Padres in 1969. When lifelong mentor and unofficial spiritual guru Lefty Phillips was named California manager for the 1970 season, Sparky made the switch to the Angels.

He never got the chance to put that Angel halo on his head. In one of those magical moments of fate, Sparky's career took a U-turn that not only changed his life, but also baseball's record books.

Borrowing a phrase from one of movies' most celebrated Italian-American anti-heroes, Sparky received "an offer he couldn't refuse."

It happened suddenly and unexpectedly on a typical autumn California day in October, 1969.

Sparky and Phillips had returned from lunch to the office of California Angels General Manager Dick Walsh. The three were discussing the possibility of trading for outfielder Alex Johnson when Walsh received a phone call. After hanging up the phone, he looked directly at Sparky.

"Do you want to manage the Cincinnati Reds?" Walsh asked.

The Cincinnati job was open, but the Reds had not tipped their hand on the candidates they were considering.

"Dick, please don't joke about something like that," Sparky replied.

"I'm not kidding," Walsh said. "That was Bob Howsam (general manager of the Reds) on the phone. You're going to be their new manager. You better give him a call."

Sparky drove to Phillips' house to call Howsam. By one of Howsam's questions regarding a Cincinnati pitcher named Jim Maloney, Sparky felt for sure he would not get the job.

"What would you do if a star pitcher decided to leave the field and just walk into the clubhouse?" Howsam asked.

"Mr. Howsam," Sparky replied. "I would very much like to answer that question. But if I did, I'd be lying because I have no idea in the world how I would ever handle anything until I'm there. If I'm not there on the spot, I can't tell you how I'd do it. All I can say is that I can guarantee you, it will get done. And it will get done right."

There was a little hesitation from Howsam. Sparky thought he did not like his answer.

"Do we have a deal?" Howsam asked. "What do you want?"

Walsh had suggested that Sparky ask for $35,000, which was a high figure for a first year manager in those days. Howsam countered with $28,500.

"Do we have a deal?" Howsam asked.

"We have a deal," Sparky replied.

"All right, you're the new manager of the Cincinnati Reds," Howsam said.

Sparky thought he had heard Howsam correctly. He just had trouble believing what he had heard.

The Reds arranged for Sparky to fly to Cincinnati that evening for a press conference the next morning. The day after the press conference, a headline in *The Cincinnati Post* read: "SPARKY WHO?"

Certainly the headline was appropriate. The new manager of the promising Cincinnati Reds was a thirty-five-year-old lifelong minor leaguer. Nobody knew who George Anderson was. And this Sparky character sounded more like a cartoon.

Even Sparky had no idea he was being considered for the job. The Reds had not yet exploded into prominence. But they were next up on the launching pad.

They were loaded with young talent and just a step away from erupting into nationwide notoriety.

"All I could figure is that when I played in Philadelphia, we won 60 games," Sparky said. "When I coached at San Diego, the Padres won 50 games. Bob must have figured I had only 110 wins on my side in the major leagues so I had to have a whole lot more hidden somewhere inside of me."

Howsam was an uncompromising leader and a strict disciplinarian. He was excruciatingly faithful to detail. He combined exacting business principles with a sensitive feel for the game. He analyzed each situation with meticulous care.

"I had decided to replace Dave Bristol as manager," Howsam explained. "I liked Dave, but I thought he had reached a peak at taking my club any higher. We kicked around a number of names. I even checked on some. It got to Sparky's name.

"A few years before, Sparky managed a Class A club at Rock Hill for me when I was general manager of the St. Louis Cardinals. Sparky had tremendous spirit and fight. He had great work habits. He loved baseball. I wouldn't say it was a gamble to hire him because I knew what he could do. I remember the "Sparky Who?" headline. Everybody found out Sparky who."

So in spite of the shock to the baseball establishment, Sparky Anderson was off on a career at Cincinnati that didn't end until he set the franchise record of 863 victories. They went along with two World Championships and four National League pennants in a span of nine years.

"Sparky was a tremendous manager," said Dick Wagner who was the Reds' business manager when Sparky was hired. He later became general manager and fired Sparky after the 1978 season.

"He worked hard at it. He threw himself into the game. He was the eternal optimist and would do just about anything the club asked him in appearances and dealing with the media. It's hard to find fault with him. He's a remarkable person. He always talked about his roots and where he came from. He never forgot what it took to get to the big leagues and the responsibilities that went along with it."

One of the first things Sparky did after becoming manager was to hire George Scherger as a coach. Scherger had been Sparky's first professional manager at Santa Barbara in 1953.

"We were both in the minor leagues when he told me he was going to manage in the big leagues one day," Scherger recalled. "He said when he got there, he wanted me as a coach. When he called, I told him I didn't want to hold him to that promise. I was a minor leaguer my whole life. I didn't think I had any business going to the bigs. But that's the kind of guy he is. He never broke a promise."

While Sparky's honesty was beyond reproach, at times his exuberance allowed his foot to tickle his tonsils. Before his first season, for instance, Sparky told all the coaches the 1970 Reds would win the division by ten games.

"I was crazy," Sparky said. "I learned fast never to make a statement like that again."

No manager makes a statement that sets up so much pressure. Of course, how many other managers can fill up a telephone book worth of words like Sparky?

"He was a feisty son of a gun," Scherger said. "He was that way as a kid when he was playing and he stayed that way as a manager in the big leagues. He talked a lot. But all he wanted to do was win."

The Reds covered Sparky's promise with room to spare. After winning 70 of their first 100 games, they won the division by 13½ games. They defeated Pittsburgh in the Playoffs and lost the World Series to Baltimore in five games.

The Reds had a gold mine of talent that would eventually develop into The Big Red Machine. They were young, however, and needed to mature. At one point early in Sparky's tenure they featured eight rookies.

Once they ripened, there was no other team like them during the decade of the '70s. During Sparky's nine years, the Reds averaged 96 wins a season. Because of the team's colorful characters, The Big Red Machine became a household name.

From those teams, Johnny Bench and Joe Morgan already have been inducted into Baseball's Hall of Fame. Tony Perez has narrowly missed getting the necessary number of votes for induction in each of the last few years. Pete Rose would have been a sure-shot first-time eligible inductee had he not been banned from the ballot because of certain off-field activities related to gambling.

"We had talent, no question about it," Bench said. "In fact, I used to joke with Sparky that if he kept his feet in the aisle and didn't trip anyone, we'd make him a star.

"But what you've got to understand is that Sparky made it enjoyable to play. He helped to put that team together. We played for him. He was the man. He had a mutual love and respect for the way we loved the game and the way we went about it."

Bench is among the most vocal of the Reds who scoffs at the suggestion that anyone could have managed those Reds.

"I think we helped to manage ourselves," Bench said. "We respected Sparky so much that we wanted to play for him. I think it was a situation where we had so many egos we could have gone the other way. You need to have someone in control. Sparky was that man.

"When you have a group of players with the stature we had who never complained, never criticized the manager, never took a shot at him . . . that is respect. I don't know if any other manager could have done that. That's the number one compliment any manager can receive . . . that you want to play for him."

That's the difference between a good manager and a great one.

"They can talk about Vince Lombardi or all the great managers in baseball," Bench said. "I wouldn't trade my chance to play for Sparky Anderson for any of them."

The Reds established themselves as the team by which excellence is measured. They won the National League West Division in five of Sparky's first seven seasons. Their back-to-back World Championships were capped by a four-game sweep over the storied New York Yankees in 1976.

Their dominance went beyond the playing field. Because of their consistent superiority, they were featured almost weekly on national television games.

The Reds of Rose, Bench, Morgan, Perez, Concepcion—and Sparky—had a charm and romance that captured the fancy of fans and media from coast to coast. They justifiably had enormous egos. They were well aware of their talent. And they knew how to treat it.

"That was the thing about Sparky," Rose explained. "He always preached to us about treating other people the way we want to be treated. He didn't make an enemy out of the press. He used it. And he taught us how to use it."

As ferociously as the Reds destroyed their enemies on the field, they were equally impressive away from the park. They spoke and dressed like professionals. They carried a businesslike demeanor.

"I remember one year when we were getting ready to go to the Playoffs," Rose recalled. "Those were the days when we ended the season on a Sunday and the Playoffs started the next weekend. We had the whole week off and we were going to fly to Pittsburgh on Thursday.

"On Wednesday, Bench and I came in with fresh haircuts. We had two guys on the team named Ted Uhlaender and Joe Hague. Sparky called me and Bench into his office and then sent the clubhouse guy for those two guys.

"They hadn't shaved in four days and it showed. Sparky was real nice. He said, 'Gentlemen, I just want to tell you—these two guys sitting in this office are very important to what we do in Pittsburgh. And you are, too. However, if you guys ain't shaved by the time that plane is ready to leave tomorrow, don't bother to show up because you ain't getting on.'

"They didn't say a word. They both got up and walked straight into the bathroom and shaved immediately. Sparky made his point. He wasn't nasty. But he wouldn't have taken them. Little things like that mattered to him. That's why we respected him."

The most talented team quickly becomes average without discipline. Sparky was grateful for the machine he had helped to build. He was not going to let a lack of discipline make the parts fly out of control.

"You're fortunate in life first if you have great parents and, secondly, if you truly enjoy the atmosphere of your work place," Bench said. "That atmosphere comes partly from the boss and partly from the people surrounding you. That's what Sparky brought to Cincinnati.

"Sparky was fortunate, too. He came in and knew how to make the most of it. He was smart enough—even though Casey Stengel lives within him—to recognize the situation, grasp it and then be in complete control."

It's easy to be in control when everything is running smoothly. The test for a leader comes when the machine starts to sputter. In the middle of Cincinnati's dominance, the Reds went into a tailspin with about a third of the season left to play.

On a Friday night in Montreal, Morgan suffered a spike wound that required a hospital visit and 17 stitches to close.

"The toughest part was spending most of the night at the hospital," Morgan explained. "We had a day game the next day and when I got back to my room, I had to ice my leg and couldn't get to sleep."

In the trainer's room the next morning, however, Morgan refuted the trainer who told him he couldn't play.

"I told him we were scuffling," Morgan said. "I had to play. I didn't even know Bench was down bad with the flu till I walked out of the trainer's room and saw him at his locker."

Morgan went into Sparky's office to tell him to put him in the lineup. Moments before, Bench had visited Sparky to let him know he wanted to play because Morgan was hurt.

Sparky was never an advocate of team meetings. He usually preferred to deal with players one-on-one.

This time was different. He hastily called a meeting. It was the perfect occasion to send a message to the rest of his struggling team.

"Boys, I got news for you," he said. "There are some of you here who don't want to play. You remind me of Cinderella waiting around for somebody to come and slide the magic slipper on your foot.

"Well let me tell you something. The slippers I got ain't gonna fit some of you guys. Because some of you don't want no part of the action. Now we've got enough guys who want to get in the fight and get a little dirty. So let me tell you what to do. Just get the hell out of the way so the real men can do their jobs."

Bench and Morgan both played. Bench homered late in the game to give the Reds a victory. Apparently the message was heard. The Reds won 45 of their last 53 games to defeat the Dodgers for the title.

"Sparky wasn't a guy who just ranted and raved," Morgan said. "When he did, the boys got the message. To be honest, it pushed me a little forward. I was going to play hard anyway. But to know he needed someone to step up, I felt like maybe I could do a little more, too.

"Sparky had a way of making everybody look in the mirror at themselves. As far as I'm concerned, that's the key to being a good manager. He forced guys to look in the mirror. Here was a case where he was bragging about me and then I looked in the mirror myself. I told myself—Joe, you need to do a little more, too. That was a big turning point for us."

Sparky had a knack for picking his spots.

"When he first came to Cincinnati he was 'Sparky Who'," Rose said. "He had been a third base coach. He never was a good player. He wasn't a well-known commodity to say the least.

"So I went to him one day and said, 'Listen. I make the most money on this team. I've been here the longest. If you ever need to get their attention—and then I kidded him because I said I know it might be a long time before I screw up on the field—you criticize me in front of the meeting. That'll get their attention and you won't lose me as a player.'

"Well, I threw to the wrong base in a spring training game just before the season started. The next night he held a meeting and said, 'We've got to quit making stupid mistakes. Rose, what the hell were you doing throwing behind the runner on that one play? How long do you have to be in the game before you learn the right way to play?'

"The guys were shocked. They figured I'd won batting titles and an MVP and this little guy is ripping him, so Rose must respect him. Everything started to fall into place after that and we started to win."

Sparky didn't just rip Rose. He actually put it to "music." In the middle of his timely tirade, he fired a couple of trash cans around the room. Garbage sailed everywhere. But the message stuck with everyone.

Walking up the tunnel to the field for the game, someone patted Sparky on the rear and whispered, "Let's go get 'em tonight, Skip."

It was Rose.

"We had a remarkably talented team," Bench said. "But Sparky was the catalyst. I can't say I give more credit to him than my father. But I look at Sparky as a father figure and friend. He believed in playing the game the right way. He believed in acting the right way. He set images and roles. When somebody gives you that, you carry it along the rest of your life."

Those kinds of things mean more than championships.

About Discipline

I don't know if anyone can really appreciate those Cincinnati teams if you never saw them play.

The numbers those teams ran up make Donald Trump numbers look like loose change. Any record book will tell you how good they were. But none of those books can really tell you why.

They could hit, run, throw, and catch the ball. They could do it forward, backward, to the side, and in their sleep. They could do everything almost on command.

Their real strength, though, was discipline. They willed themselves to win. They dared anyone to stop them.

Discipline is a mighty powerful weapon. You can fill a lot of holes if you teach yourself discipline.

Sometimes I laugh to myself when I hear some of the excuses people come up with when they're passed over for a job. When you're looking for a job, it ain't up to the boss to show you anything. It's up to you to show the boss why you're the best person. That takes discipline.

Disciplined people make mistakes, too. But they don't waste the gifts God gave them to succeed.

The Reds never wasted anything. They had so much talent they could almost toy with another team. Sometimes they had teams begging them just to let them go in peace. They were like that big ol' alleycat that played with a mouse that is fixing to die.

If you wanted to stand up and slug it out, we had the

muscle with Bench and Morgan and Perez and Foster. If you wanted to dare our running game, we'd cut loose the ropes on Morgan and Griffey and Geronimo. And Rose was running around the bases every time I looked up.

On defense we caught anything that stayed on the radar screen. With Bench and Morgan and Concepcion and Geronimo up the middle, you couldn't drop a bowling ball from ten feet in between those guys.

Except maybe for starting pitching, there wasn't one part of the game where we didn't dominate. I would have loved to seen my eight regulars playing behind a pitching staff like the Braves have now. I honestly believe we would have played .700 ball. I think one year we could have won 130 games.

That regular lineup I played as a group were the most dominant players I ever saw in my 43 years in pro ball.

What people don't understand about those Reds teams, though, never showed up in the box scores. How they carried themselves off the field is what brought it altogether once they stepped past those white lines.

Those guys were pros. They looked like pros. They acted like pros. And they played like pros.

Look at their team pictures. Then compare them to any team photo you see today. Put them side-by-side and you'll notice the difference.

Then you'll see why this was The Big Red Machine!

All of them were shaved. All of them had their hair cut neatly. When they practiced, all of them wore their uniform like they were getting ready for war. Each and every one of them wore his uniform exactly the same as the next guy.

That's discipline. Their outside appearance was a picture of what made them tick inside.

They were professionals. They were proud of who they were. They would never belittle the Cincinnati

Reds front office. They would never belittle me. And sure as hell they would never belittle themselves.

When they went on the road, they looked like the proudest and most powerful baseball team that was ever put together. When we went on a ten-day road trip, I swear Joe Morgan had a different suit for each day. You'd never catch Joe wearing the same outfit on one trip.

There's an old saying in baseball—if you look like a major leaguer then you'll play like one.

A lot of people might wonder what this has to do with winning. Baseball's no different than any walk of life. If you can't discipline yourself, how can you expect those around you to be disciplined?

Think about the education system where your kids go to school. If the teachers are off running around in a hundred different directions, it's impossible for the overall program to help those kids develop as a whole.

It's the same thing in business. If the sales department doesn't communicate with assembly, that company might wind up with more gadgets than it could give away for the next ten Christmases.

It's pure and simple discipline. Those Reds had it and were proud to show it everywhere they went.

The guys on those teams didn't totally like each other. But the discipline we developed taught them to tolerate each other so that we could get the job done together.

We had stars. But no one star was bigger than the team.

Can you imagine a doctor who thinks he's bigger than the whole hospital staff around him? You better hope he ain't the one cutting on you in the operating room because he can't do it alone without those nurses and the guy who gives you the ether.

The guys on those Reds teams tolerated each other

for seven-and-a-half months out of the year. They tolerated me. And I tolerated them.

One of the greatest strengths of any successful system is the ability of the people to tolerate the strengths and weaknesses of their fellow workers.

The Reds had so much natural talent they could play over most of their mistakes.

Nothing ain't worth nothing if it doesn't come with hard work. Even with all their talent, they had to learn how to become a truly great team.

That's what made me feel so proud. The Big Red Machine didn't just happen. There's no question we had a nucleus. But we also had a lot of young players who needed to be shaped.

Our coaches worked hard and our players weren't afraid to listen. I think that's how a principal must feel when he has a particularly gifted graduating class.

Every one of those players was special to the team in his own way. But that foursome of Morgan, Bench, Perez, and Rose, I swear came from another planet.

Every day, I never failed to learn something from all of them. Not just about baseball, but also about the importance of going about your business the right way every day.

If a manager or a teacher or any kind of boss is smart, he's gonna learn as much from the people he's leading as they're gonna learn from him. You learn how people act in certain situations. Then you make adjustments so that the next time is always better than the last.

If a person can't do one thing, maybe he can do something else. But you ain't gonna know if you don't learn from those around you.

For instance, Morgan wasn't the fastest runner I ever seen. But no one was a better base stealer. If he had been a pickpocket, they never would have caught him.

Morgan didn't wake up one day to discover he was the best. He worked hard to learn and never stopped learning when he got to the top. He made mistakes. Then he learned from those mistakes to become even better.

He kept a book on pitchers. He knew all their habits and all their moves. Joe could have led the league in stolen bases every year if he wanted to. He just knew when to pick his spots. He never wasted them. I let Joe run whenever he wanted. Everything I learned about base running I learned from Joe Morgan.

He was that smart of a player. He knew how to beat another team. Joe could be one of the best managers in the game if he ever wanted to take the job.

Bench played his position better than anybody else played theirs in the history of the game. There's only one way to explain it. God reached down and touched his mama when she was carrying him. He told her that she was going to produce the best catcher in the history of the game.

I never meant no disrespect, but one time I told the writers that the Bible talks about Christ coming again. I said I ain't too sure He wasn't crouching behind home plate in Cincinnati for all those years.

Bench knew he was good. But he wanted to be the best. I've seen a lot of people in life just skate by on talent alone. The great ones refuse to settle for just being good.

Tony Perez was not the best hitter I ever saw. Nobody was better, though, with the game on the line.

Tony did it with concentration as much as he did it with the bat. Tony has a spirit inside of him that makes him place the team ahead of Tony Perez.

Tony taught all of us the meaning of heart. He didn't get as many headlines as the other three. But he was the glue that kept all of us stuck together.

I never realized until we traded him after the 1976

World Series how much he meant to the team. It was the biggest mistake the Cincinnati Reds ever made. Bob Howsam agrees. It was a mistake by all of us. I okayed the deal and to this day I regret it. We would have won at least two more championships in a row with Tony Perez.

Tony never had no Latin or black or white in him. Tony was a man. And everybody else was a man to Tony. Imagine what a better world this would be if everyone took that attitude.

There was a calmness about Tony that kept everyone in line. He could simmer Rose down. He could simmer Bench down. He could simmer Morgan down. I never once saw Tony throw a bat or a helmet or show anger. All he ever cared about was winning. He above everyone else was the most unselfish star.

Peter Edward Rose lifted discipline to another level. He's a man like I ain't never seen before and will never see again. Mentally and physically, Peter Edward was tougher than any human being I've ever been around.

Peter Edward taught me determination. Everybody wants to be successful. But how many of us are willing to bleed for it?

If you want to beat him, then you better kill him. If you kill him, call the coroner to pronounce him dead. And even if he does, ask for a second opinion. Because if there is any way Peter Edward can breathe, he'll come back to get you.

He was a man who always thought he was eighteen years old. When you think you've run into the meanest, toughest, baddest guy . . . go one better. That's Peter Edward Rose.

He played as hard in exhibition games as he did in the World Series. The score never mattered. Peter Edward refused to give up even one time at bat.

Each year during the season, we played an exhibition game in Indianapolis. I'd start my regular lineup and then pull them out after we batted around. I was going to take Pete out after he batted once so he could get some rest.

He talked me into one more time up. He hit a liner to the outfield that fell in for a hit. Instead of stopping at first base, though, he went charging into second. He slid in under the tag and the crowd went crazy. He motioned to me in the dugout to send in a pinch runner.

When he started trotting off the field, the crowd really went wild. They cheered him like he had just won the World Series. When he got to the dugout, he winked at me.

"That's what they came to see," he cracked.

Maybe I ain't supposed to say this because baseball has banned him. But if Peter Edward Rose ain't supposed to be in the Hall of Fame, then how in the hell can they allow anybody else in there?

We had stars on those teams. And we had a lot of egos. But how in the hell can you be a star if you ain't got the ego to drive you over the edge?

If somebody says I have a big ego, that's the greatest compliment he can give. If a man has a big ego, then he's reaching for the stars. It's how he handles that ego once he gets there.

We had a lot of egos in Cincinnati and that's what I had to maneuver my way around. Those guys knew how to use it. They were proud and they knew how to get the job done.

The Reds taught me a lot more about life than they did baseball. Today I understand what discipline and dedication mean to success in all fields.

The Big Red Machine was special. I hope those guys learned as much from me as I did from them.

(Credit: George Anderson)

Sparky did have a hammer and used it for the start of a storybook managerial career in 1964 when he took over Toronto of the International League. After saying he should be fired if he didn't win the championship, his team finished fifth and . . . he was fired.

There really was a time when Sparky wore overalls and played with all the neighborhood kids. He spent his first nine years in Bridgewater, SD before his family moved to Los Angeles

Sparky's father, LeRoy, helped his son to learn baseball. But he also taught him the single most important lesson of his life which he still carries proudly today—"the one thing you can do in life is treat people nicely and it won't cost a dime."

With those rabbit ears and infectious smile, it isn't hard to pick out little Georgie Anderson who served as a batboy for some of the University of Southern California NCAA championship teams.

Sparky (left) and Billy Consolo have been friends since the fifth grade. They starred on the Dorsey (Los Angeles) High School team before moving on to the major leagues. Consolo coached for the Tigers throughout Sparky's Detroit career. Now the two are inseparable golfing partners.

Except for the white hair later, Sparky looked the same when he managed Toronto in the International League in 1964 or his last Detroit Tigers club in 1995.

In 1956, one of Sparky's Montreal teammates was another future Hall of Fame manager. That's Tommy Lasorda with his arm around Sparky. Years later, the two were spirited National League rivals with Sparky leading Cincinnati's Big Red Machine and Lasorda holding court as manager of the Los Angeles Dodgers.

Sparky actually did make it to the major leagues for one whole season. His managerial talents turned out to be a whole lot more memorable than his .218 batting average.

(Credit: AP/World Wide Photos)

Who's to say which one is prouder—Sparky as the Cincinnati Reds' all-time winningest manager or his mom and dad? Those eyes on all three tell it all.

Way back when he was just Daddy. Now Sparky's three kids realize just how important their father was to baseball history. Standing between Johnny Bench and his father is Lee. To Sparky's left are Shirlee and Albert.

One George always listened to the other George when Sparky managed Cincinnati. Sparky called George Scherger one of the brightest and most intense competitors he had ever encountered in baseball. Sparky kept his promise to make the lifelong minor league manager a coach in the majors, once he got the chance.

They left their mark—in bold red—forever on baseball's record books—The Big Red Machine. How about laying this lineup on your worst enemy? From the left—Pete Rose, Joe Morgan, Johnny Bench, Tony Perez, George Foster, Dave Concepcion, Ken Griffey and Cesar Geronimo.

(Credits: Bettmann Archives)

Sparky was blessed with a pair of aces for short-stops—Dave Concepcion at Cincinnati and Alan Trammell at Detroit. Sparky knew the talent was there. It was his job to shape their character and teach his prize youngsters the responsibilities of living the right way.

(Credit: AP/World Wide Photos)

The 1975 World Series between the Cincinnati Reds and the Boston Red Sox is considered the most memorable of modern times. When it was finally finished, Sparky and his boys took home the prize—the World Championship trophy. It was the first of three in Sparky's career.

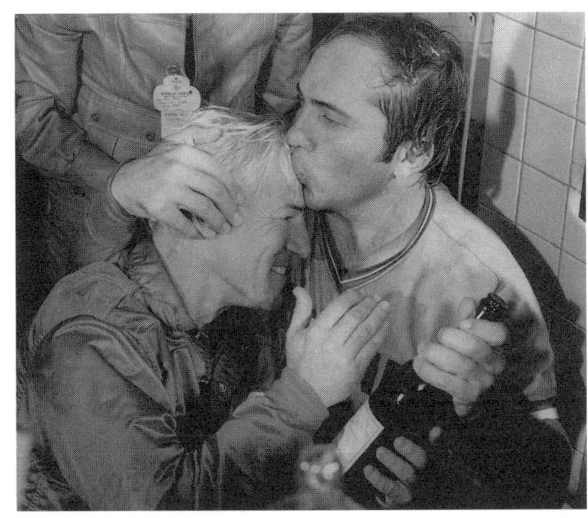

A bottle of champagne and a kiss on the head from Hall of Fame catcher Johnny Bench. Does it get any better after winning a World Series?

(Credit: Bettmann Archives)

If sheer determination can move a mountain, save the excavation truck and get these two guys. In baseball's long and storied history, there's only been one Sparky and one Pete Rose.

(Credit: AP/World Wide Photos)

Even as a young manager at Cincinnati, Sparky believed each player had to be handled individually. That included such stars as Joe Morgan (stretching) and Pete Rose.

Alan Trammell still believes that Sparky never missed one move that his players made. "He was like a high school principal," Trammell said. Sparky was always concerned that his boys mature as men as well as ballplayers.

Only the hairstyles have changed. Sparky and Carol were sweethearts since junior high. They've been happily married since 1953.

Although Carol and George prefer evenings eating a sandwich in front of the TV, once in awhile there is a special occasion to attend. And they make a stunning couple!

No reporter ever had a greater friend than Sparky. He speaks his own language that fills empty tapes and makes a writer scramble for an extra notepad. A camera has yet to be invented that doesn't love Sparky.

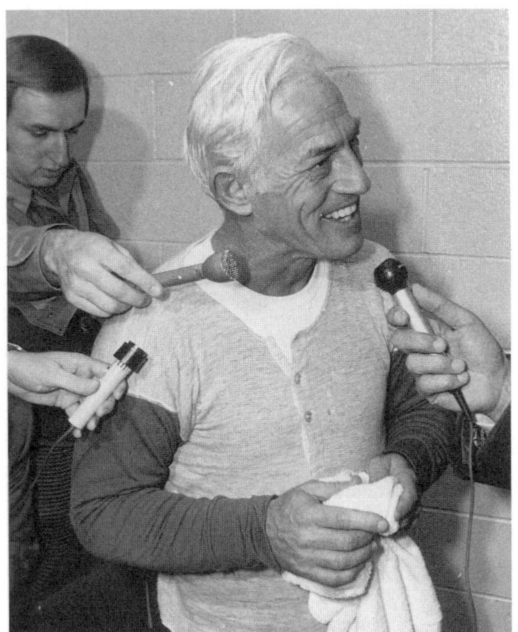

(Credit: AP/World Wide Photos)

(Credit: AP/World Wide Photos)

Although he never wears them, Sparky has collected three World Championship rings. He's the only manager in history to have won a World Series in both leagues. He also has two National League Championship rings and five from the All-Star Games.

Bo and Sparky are two legitimate single-name sports celebrities. When Bo served as Tiger president, Sparky learned first-hand how much alike the two really are in their concern for doing things honestly and with integrity.

It's hard to believe there ever was a tighter relationship between manager and general manager of a baseball team than there was between Sparky and the late Jim Campbell, who brought him to Detroit. They were a powerful team and shared an equally rich friendship.

If it weren't for Lefty Phillips, there might not be a Sparky today. It was Lefty who doggedly taught Sparky all the nuances of the game and signed him to his first professional contract. Sparky claims he owes his three World Championship rings to Lefty.

Neither knows exactly how or why, but somehow George McCarthy and Sparky struck up a friendship that has enriched the lives of both. Sparky used to bring "young" Georgie (now over 90) to spring training where both learned a little bit more about life from each other.

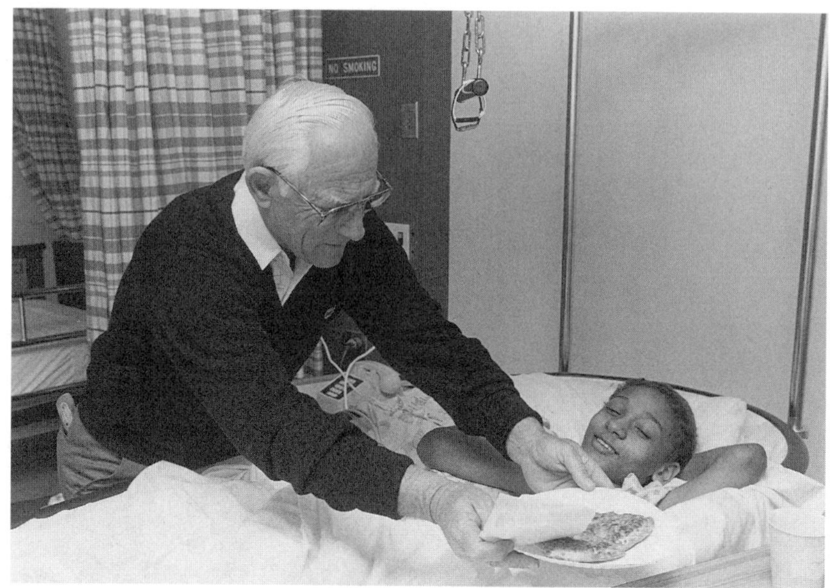

If there was one thing Sparky loved more than a two-out ninth inning rally, it was sharing precious moments with hospitalized kids in Detroit and Cincinnati. No one truly appreciates how much time he dedicated to his secret passion.

Sparky will forever be remembered for his baseball records. He takes even greater pride in CATCH—the charity he created to help hospitalized children in Detroit. The little girl Sparky is holding later died from AIDS.

(Credit: Allsport Photos)

A leader must have the courage to make decisions regardless of how lonely it makes him feel. When Sparky made that decision, nothing could change his mind. Not the opposition . . . not his own players . . . not the fans . . . nothing.

Just Keep Going

Winston Churchill once said, "When you're going through hell, keep going."

The best way to keep from getting burned is to somehow fight your way out of the fire.

The perils of baseball, of course, don't compare to those faced by Churchill and the rest of the world at war a half century ago.

But until October 22, 1975, Sparky agonized in his own hell of self doubt.

Since 1970, the Cincinnati Reds certainly had established themselves as one of the most feared weapons of baseball war. Until they won their final battle of 1975, though, Sparky was fearful the Reds might become baseball's most beautiful bridesmaid.

Among officials and fans across the country, the Reds of the '70s were generally regarded as baseball's 600-pound gorilla. They had assembled the finest collection of legalized bashers, bruisers and all-around bullies anyone had seen since the glory years of the Yankees.

They were loaded with talent. There was only one hole. They couldn't win the big one after waltzing through the National League all summer long.

They made it to the World Series in 1970 only to lose to the Baltimore Orioles in five games. They returned to the Series in 1972. This time they were edged by the Oakland Athletics in seven games.

In 1973, the Reds never made it to the Series. Despite being overwhelming favorites to defeat New York in the National League Playoffs, the upstart Mets ignored the Goliath from the Midwest to upset the Reds in five games.

The Reds were close to becoming an enigma. They made it to the dance, but could never get that midnight kiss.

In 1975, the Reds left their mark on history. And it was so incredibly appropriate for it to occur in what most observers agree is the most memorable World Series of modern times.

For the baseball purist, the 1972 Series with Oakland was played almost flawlessly. From an overall national perspective, the 1975 Series was sheer poetry for drama, color, and romance.

Even lukewarm fans were moved by the spectacle.

It was the World Series that transcended baseball. It evolved into an unexpected network television miniseries. It mesmerized all segments of American society and had them wishing it would never end.

The Big Red Machine collided with the Boston Red Sox and all of their New England charm.

Destiny usually has a cast of heroes in waiting. Other times, it seems, some heroes write histories of their own.

The most unlikely of heroes had to be this character called Sparky. He was the little guy next door who scrapped his way to the throne of America's national sport.

It can be argued that Sparky was in the right place at the right time. Destiny placed him to inherit a team on the brink of greatness. Unlike some who throw away a gift with the wrapping paper, he meticulously turned that gift into a treasure.

He "kept on going" right through his personal hell of showdown defeats.

The Reds punctuated their place in history in 1976 when they manhandled the storied Yankees in four straight games for their second straight World Championship. Their march through New York solidified The Big Red Machine's niche of baseball legend.

It was that 1975 storybook drama, though, that still remains the World Series' contribution to Americana.

Following an endless string of spectacular plays and a

three-day delay because of a Northeaster running up the Coast, the Reds rallied to victory with two-out in the ninth inning of Game Seven.

That three-day delay captured the imagination of TV network news. It piqued a national anticipation for the final two games. For Sparky, the delay was worse than a needle in the left eye. At the end, however, the stigma of the perpetual bridesmaid finally was dashed.

It didn't come easy. Nothing good ever does. In fact, an erroneous piece of history from the post-seventh game celebration at Boston's Fenway Park still makes Sparky smile.

Celebrated sports artist Leroy Neiman captured the Reds' triumph as players and coaches frolicked near the pitcher's mound after the game-ending out. In the painting, Sparky is pictured as part of the raucous celebration.

Sparky, in fact, was nowhere to be seen. He had scampered up the runway which connects the dugout to the visitors' clubhouse. For a few precious moments, he sat alone on the third step before greeting his players at the locker room door.

Quickly and quietly, he thanked God. He also thanked his mother and father, people like Lefty Phillips and anyone who played the littlest part in making the moment possible.

Even if he had wanted to join his players on the field, Sparky was helpless to make it. He had spent all of his strength getting to the finish line. To join the clubhouse party and handle the onslaught of media which he normally managed with ease, he had to steal some energy away from next day's reserve.

After dragging himself into his office, he received a congratulatory phone call from Red Sox legend Tom Yawkey.

"Thank you, Mr. Yawkey," Sparky told the venerable owner. "But baseball was the winner in this World Series. This one was so great for the game. It belongs to the fans more than it does to the Reds or Red Sox."

That captured the spirit succinctly. It was the Series that America had won.

For reasons not totally explainable, that Series spun a magic of its own. Each dramatic moment was captured magnificently by television and still cameras from every conceivable angle. So many images still remain alive today. They're indelibly etched into our memories like living snapshots captured for all time.

The most vivid is the miraculous finish to Game Six. It's the picture of Boston catcher Carlton Fisk frantically hopping down the first base line.

With his arms waving high above his head, Fisk tries to coax his long fly ball down the left field line to stay in fair territory. The 12th inning drive struck the foul pole above Fenway's famous green wall to snap a 6-6 tie and send the Series to a deciding seventh game.

"I didn't know how it would happen, I just knew something bad was gonna happen," Sparky reflected on the home run that is shown even today on most baseball highlight films and promotional spots. "After what happened in the eighth inning, I could feel the devil getting ready to poke his pitchfork."

What happened in the eighth inning was a Boston home run even more unlikely than Fisk's. This one came with two outs from pinch hitter Bernie Carbo. He tied the game with a three-run drive over the center field fence.

Carbo's shot came after two quick strikes. It also came immediately after Sparky talked himself out of making a pitching change to seal the victory.

Sparky failed to make that change. And the Reds had to wait another 24 hours for vindication.

"I knew (Will) McEnaney could strike him out," Sparky explained. McEnaney was the left-handed pitcher Sparky had warming up.

"I took one step up the dugout steps then spun around and went back down," Sparky continued. "I have no idea why I did that. I had never done that before and never did it again. Right there, though, I thought I cost us the World Series."

When Fenway finally cleared after Game Six, it seemed like all of New England had jammed the streets around the historic park. In the desolate quiet under the stands, Sparky slowly walked to the team bus.

"Wasn't that some kind of game?" bubbled Pete Rose who caught up with Sparky on his way to the bus. "That was the best game I ever played in."

Sparky looked at Rose like Ebenezer Scrooge must have looked at the ghost of Christmas Future.

"Are you nuts?" asked Sparky who was so exhausted he must have thought he was hallucinating. "I just lost us the World Series and you're telling me that's the best game you ever played in?"

Always the bully, Rose looked Sparky in the eye.

"This will always be remembered as one of the greatest games in history," Rose said. "And we were part of it. We're gonna win this thing tomorrow."

If Sparky had tried to teach confidence in his players, he received the lesson of his lifetime from one of his own. Rose had just promised victory. Somehow, though, Sparky wasn't yet convinced.

Sparky spent a sleepless night. But the lesson slowly seeped into place. If something is worth keeping for eternity, then it doesn't matter what price must be paid.

"I didn't know how it was gonna happen," Sparky said, "but I just knew we were gonna win. So what if we had to play another game. I knew we were the better team. We just needed to stay confident. We needed to play our normal game."

It took all nine innings before Sparky could truly relax. Joe Morgan delivered the game-winning hit with two-out in the ninth. Perhaps a little short of folklore status, the 1975 seven-game drama still rates at the top of World Series history.

It took Sparky a couple of dances in the Series to learn how never to underestimate an opponent.

In 1970 and again in 1972, the Reds' visits to the World Series were accompanied by an overconfident Sparky. Certainly his exuberance had become part of his charm.

Both times, however, he found a way to stick one of his spikes halfway down his throat.

After sweeping three straight games from the hard-hitting Pirates to win the National League Playoffs in 1970,

Sparky proclaimed to the media that the Reds already had beaten the best team in baseball. Baltimore, apparently, quietly differed. They beat the Reds in five games.

The Reds had to rally to beat the Pirates in five games for the 1972 National League crown.

Not to be outdone, Sparky reiterated his opinion of National League superiority. Again he sent his spike down a familiar path past his tonsils.

"Cincinnati and Pittsburgh are the two best teams in baseball," he said to a group of writers before the World Series began. "We beat the Pirates in the Playoffs. That sort of makes the World Series anticlimactic."

While the Reds pushed it to seven games, Oakland persevered. Finally Sparky had learned his lesson. Again . . . the hard way.

For the next three years, the haunting never stopped. Not until after the last out of the 1975 classic when he was quietly giving thanks did he finally feel redeemed.

The purity of persistence is in its practice. So when going through hell . . . just keep going.

Refusing to Quit

Except for spitting and telling a lie, there ain't nothing easier to do than quit.

Quitting is for losers. Cowards never win. Getting beat don't make you a loser. How you handle defeat is the real measure of a person.

That's why that 1975 team will always be so special to me. The 1976 club was even more talented. But that first championship is always the sweetest.

It showed everybody in the country that those Reds did not quit. That wouldda been too easy after our first two trips to the Series.

Always being the favorite ain't exactly the best seat in the house. That bull's-eye on your back gets awfully heavy. People are less forgiving of those who are expected to succeed day after day.

We had talent. I think we had the best team in the game. Even the best sometimes trip on their way to the cookie jar. The difference between a champion and a good team is that the champion keeps getting up . . . and eventually grabs all the cookies.

If sports truly are the mirrors of life, then The Big Red Machine ain't a bad bunch to hang on the wall.

I admire the school kid who just squeaked onto the honor roll but studies till it gets light outside so he can get all "A's." I admire the father or the mother who has to work 12 hours a day to pay all the bills and still makes time to spend with their kids.

Those people ain't quitters. They don't show up on television. They don't get no headlines. But all of them are champions in their own quiet way.

We get too many of the headlines in sports. Maybe that's the way it's supposed to be. Once in a while, though, let's remember the lessons that sports are supposed to teach us.

We don't need to stand up and cheer the mailman for bringing us letters every day. But every so often, let's appreciate the little guy who does his job the best way he knows how.

I learned plenty of lessons from my trips to the World Series. One of the most important was to get my tongue out of the way of my brain.

The first two times we made it, I said a couple of things I probably should have swallowed before they got past my teeth. I didn't mean no disrespect to the Orioles or the Athletics when I said we already had beaten the best.

In fact, I was having some fun. I was just trying to put some life into the game. If you can't have fun in baseball, you might as well pack up all the bats and balls and head for the fishing hole.

Maybe it was a mistake, but I didn't mean no harm. It gave all the press something to write about. And they wrote more words about it than I ever said.

When we made it in 1975, though, I tiptoed around comparing the Reds and the Red Sox. I made it sound like we were just happy to be there.

The World Series is Christmas and prom night and wedding day and New Year's Eve all wrapped into one.

It makes your stomach jumpy. You could juggle three eggs on it. It throws you all the way back in time to when you were just a boy.

There ain't no sporting event like the World Series. For that week to ten days, you're up there on a national stage.

When we played in those Series, everything we said was plastered in newspapers across the country. Everything we did was seen in living rooms all over the world.

At a World Series the media swallows you up. You play pinball with all the people just to get from the dugout to the field. You can't tie your shoe without someone asking why you use a right-hand loop instead of a left-hand one.

I love the media. For someone who ain't been through a Series, though, it's impossible to understand how big the whole thing is.

If you're lucky enough to make it to the World Series, the only good one is the one that you win. A bridesmaid might look pretty. But nobody remembers anybody but the bride.

In 1975 we really became a soap opera. That Series ballooned into something bigger than baseball.

Part of it was The Big Red Machine. Part was the Red Sox and all that New England charm. I never had so much fun visiting a city in a Series as I did in Boston.

I think the weather threw the Series into a whole new dimension. After five great games and then a three-day rain delay, the buildup for the rest of the Series got bigger than the coming of Santa Claus.

The story bounced from the sports pages to the nightly national news.

We couldda turned out to be the biggest flop since the Titanic. But then that Game Six jumped up like Elvis at the senior dance.

Rose was right. That might have been the best game in World Series history.

Losing ain't never fun. But that did teach me how important confidence really is. No one goes anywhere in life without talent. No one becomes a champion, though, without confidence.

A doctor might be a terrific surgeon. But I don't want him cutting on me if he ain't sure of himself.

Any kid who watched that seventh game had to walk away with something he can still use as an adult. If the roof is leaking, you can still save the house if you have enough confidence that you can plug the hole.

It gets back to not quitting. There are times when everyone simply has to refuse to give up. Maybe times are tough at work. Maybe the mortgage payment is two months behind.

You ain't gonna win by quitting. But if you ain't afraid to dig just a little bit deeper, you just might find a way.

That one game did more for baseball than all the advertising and promotions all the money in the world could buy. For those who paid close attention, they learned a few things to help them get through some rough spots in life.

I think some fans who started to drift away from the game got hooked and came back. The whole Series made fans out of some people who never really followed the game.

The 1976 Reds team was better. The 1975 experience, though, had a life of its own.

Managing in a World Series is a privilege. There are a lot of good managers who spend a career without making it.

There's a lot more to learn from the experience than just who wins the games. Both teams in that 1975 Series showed the fans that anything is possible if people simply learn not to quit.

The Reds' Pink Slip

Only two years after the city of Cincinnati celebrated its second straight World Championship, baseball fans there again rallied together.

This time it was for something they were losing rather than embracing.

On November 27, 1978, Cincinnati was stunned. Sparky Anderson unexpectedly was fired as manager of the Reds.

In most major league cities, many fans clamor for a manager's scalp even before he's actually dismissed. The scene in Cincinnati was different. Even lukewarm fans there had become accustomed to that white hair on Sparky's head.

Not only was he the leader, Sparky actually had become the trademark of The Big Red Machine. Sparky made people feel proud of the Reds and their city. His infectious bubbly personality also made them feel good about themselves.

After the shocking announcement, various media outlets quickly conducted phone-in polls to measure fan reaction of the controversial move.

More than 80% of the respondents were outraged that Sparky had been fired. Some more militant fans, in fact, made a dummy to look like General Manager Dick Wagner. They hung it in effigy outside of Riverfront Stadium.

Although Cincinnati finished second to the Dodgers by just two-and-a-half games that season, The Big Red Machine was slowly being dismantled. Tony Perez had been traded after the 1976 season. Pete Rose signed as a free agent with the Phillies for the 1979 season.

And now Sparky was gone.

As with most dismissals, the final decision was probably

the result of a combination of factors. The bottom line was that Sparky no longer was part of the team he thought he would be with for life.

Sparky believes that one of the factors that led to his firing was his refusal to approve certain coaching replacements that the Reds wished to make. He would not agree to the dismissal of pitching coach Larry Shepard and third base coach Alex Grammas.

"They would have to fire me first before they let any of my coaches go," Sparky said. "I was not gonna let that happen. We finished second in 1977 and 1978. I wasn't gonna lay the blame on two guys."

Actually, injuries did more to undermine the Reds of 1978 than any other factor. Joe Morgan was limited to 132 of the 162-game schedule. Johnny Bench appeared in only 120. And the Reds still finished second to the Dodgers by only a nose.

Things were changing in Cincinnati. One of the nation's most conservative Midwest cities had suddenly become radical with its ball club.

"A person can have a job for too long," said Bob Howsam the former general manager of the Reds who hired Sparky as manager in October 1969. Howsam retired from the position before the 1978 season. He remained with the club as a consultant and Wagner assumed the job of general manager.

"A person can get complacent," Howsam continued. "I think the whole organization got complacent in 1977. I, unfortunately, traded Perez away. I wanted to keep my club a little younger. Perez and Dan Driessen wanted to play first base. I should have let them fight it out. But I had so much respect for Perez, I figured it was best to trade him. I thought I was helping him.

"When I look back, I think I got complacent. From the top all the way down, we got complacent. We thought we could win just by walking out on the field."

Other factors led to the departure of Sparky. It was the beginning of the era of player free agent madness. Multiyear million dollar contracts were being handed out like Monopoly money.

"Sparky still thinks Bob Howsam made the decision to

make a change," Wagner said. "It was my decision. I love Sparky. He's a tremendous human being. I could not get across to him the big change in the players with their agents and that they could leave the club. We had a lot of good young players and I was afraid we'd lose them if they didn't get a chance to play.

"Some of his ideas were screwy, but Sparky always came up with a lot of them. He was always so enthusiastic. He bubbled from morning to night. He was good for the game and still is good for the game."

Like most of the fans, the Cincinnati players were stunned and dismayed over Sparky's dismissal.

"The thing that got him fired was, supposedly, he didn't communicate with the younger players," Bench said. "That came from questions being asked by the general manager of how the players felt.

"I think some of the kids didn't think they were getting enough playing time. It didn't matter to Sparky. If you deserved to play, you played. Not everyone can play. Sparky's objective was to get the very best team on the field. There's always one or two people who aren't satisfied. That's not the manager's fault."

Nevertheless, for a combination of reasons, the once "Sparky Who" that forged his way to single-name celebrity was now "Sparky Gone."

It happened a few days after the Reds had returned from a goodwill baseball trip to Japan. Wagner visited Sparky in Los Angeles. Sparky was under the impression the meeting had been called to discuss the possible free agent signings of pitcher Tommy John and outfielder Lee Lacy.

Sparky and Wagner met in Room 1118 of the Marriott Hotel at the Los Angeles airport.

"Every time I drive by the hotel I think of that room," Sparky now jokes.

Wagner returned to Cincinnati to announce the move the next morning. For the next three days, activity at the Anderson home resembled a Monday morning at the New York Stock Exchange. At the time, the Andersons had two telephone lines in their home. Each rang constantly. Carol and daughter Shirlee answered all of them. They carefully made a long list. Between radio and television interviews, Sparky returned all calls.

The U.S. Post Office delivered two overstuffed mail sacks of letters from around the country. Again, overwhelmingly, fans expressed their outrage. They thanked Sparky for all those wonderful years.

"It was so busy that I didn't have time to really understand what had happened," Sparky explained. "Actually, it was sort of like a party atmosphere. It was kind of fun. I never dreamed so many people could get upset over the Reds firing me."

Activity around the Anderson household became numbing. It wasn't until years later that Sparky's daughter, Shirlee, truly appreciated the manner in which her father handled the affair.

"I was just out of high school when he got fired," Shirlee recalled. "Then one day it hit me. The way he handled it was beautiful. He was hurt and it wasn't easy for him. All he told the reporters, though, is that he understood. He never once pointed the finger at anybody or said anything bad.

"I had three wonderful children from my first husband before he walked out. I told myself that no matter what he did and how much it hurt, I had to be the bigger person. Those kids didn't need to hear me saying anything bad about their father.

"I learned that from my father. Dad held his head high and he became a bigger person. I was so proud of the way he handled that. I'll carry that for the rest of my life."

One of the first callers to reach Sparky after the firing was Morgan. The Hall of Fame second baseman fumed over the Reds' decision before Sparky calmed him down.

"Little man, we are friends and I know you're upset," Sparky said. "Now you've got a job to do and I want you to do it with the same class you've always shown. You play just as hard for the new man as you did for me."

Morgan had been informed about the move through a call from Wagner at about 6 a.m. (Pacific time) prior to the announcement. Morgan was so shocked, he simply hung up the phone. He immediately called Sparky to find out if he had been dreaming.

"Sparky's firing was wrong and to this day, I don't understand it," Morgan said. "Sparky asked me not to say too much and for all of us to handle it with class.

"They used him to go to Japan. They fired him when he got back. They used him because they didn't want to take a new manager over there with The Big Red Machine. Now when he comes back, they fire him. If he wasn't good enough the day the season ended, that's when they should have fired him. That irritated me. They didn't do it with class."

The dismissal was particularly painful to Morgan who enjoyed a special relationship with Sparky.

"It was difficult for me because we didn't have just a manager/player relationship," Morgan said. "It was like somebody had done something to my family."

Sparky also received calls from Bench, Rose, several managers and various other baseball dignitaries.

When the party finally died, though, an obsession started to brew within Sparky. He wanted to return to baseball to show the Reds they had made a mistake.

Within the first month, Sparky received six different offers to manage. He thanked each club, but told them he had decided to sit out one year before making a decision.

"One guy told me I was like an apple that had fallen from the tree," Sparky said. "He had a first-year manager and I told him to give the young man a chance.

"I knew what he meant by a fallen apple. It was the first time in my life that I knew in my heart that I was a real part of the baseball tree. I knew I could go back to work in baseball any time I wanted."

At baseball's winter meetings that December, Kansas City Manager Whitey Herzog had a message for the rest of his colleagues.

"Boys, you better get off to a quick start," Herzog said. "There's a white-haired guy sitting out in California and every owner has his telephone number."

Looking back, Sparky says getting fired from Cincinnati was one of the best things that ever happened to him. At the time, however, he felt as though he had been booted out of a family reunion.

"I was at a dinner in Los Angeles with Tiger owner John Fetzer and his general manager, Jim Campbell, shortly after the Tigers hired Sparky," Howsam said. "I remember Mr. Fetzer said that if Sparky could manage for Bob Howsam, he was good enough to manage for him.

"I cannot speak too highly of Sparky Anderson. He's a man's man and a player's player. He wanted to do what was right all the time. He's a good family man and a good religious man. He's just an outstanding person."

It simply was time for Sparky to move on from Cincinnati. It didn't take long for him to find another home.

Soon he would be in Detroit where he would double the length of his stay in Cincinnati. He eventually would establish the Detroit franchise record for victories as he had in Cincinnati.

And he would vindicate the dismissal that ultimately became the springboard for some of his greatest glories.

A firing in baseball, as with all professions, is what the individual makes of it. It's only a defeat if it's allowed to be. Handled with class, it often is the key to a much brighter future.

Turning Defeat into Victory

The sure cure for vanity is the water bucket test.

It works for presidents the same way it works for shoe shine boys.

If you ever think you're too big to be replaced, get yourself a bucket and fill it with water. Make a fist and punch all the way down. Then pull your fist out and see how quickly that hole gets filled.

That, right there, will prove to you that there's no irreplaceable man.

There were a lot of wrinkles that went into the mix when I got fired in Cincinnati. To be perfectly honest, I have to admit that I probably got a little bigger than anybody should allow himself to get.

That was my fault. I think that happens to all of us when there's been a lot of success.

I made some demands that maybe I shouldn't have made. If I had to do it over again, I would have done things a little different. But like they always say—give me a second putt and I'll sink it all the time.

The trick is to do it right the first time. That's what I want every young person to realize as soon as they can. Make the right decision the first time and you don't have to play no "what if" games.

There ain't nobody bigger than the system. Take that from somebody who found out firsthand.

It don't matter if you're in baseball or working in a hospital or flipping pancakes in "Grits and Grease." It's all the same thing. There ain't no rose that's prettier than the bush it comes from.

I was no different than anyone else. I could say it was all their fault, but that would be wrong. It was partly theirs and partly mine. Most every split is a fifty-fifty deal. If anyone deserves a kick in the butt more than the other, it was me.

We had some differences. But had I looked at the situation and examined where the roadblocks were, I think they couldda been worked out without going to war.

I went to war. And guess who finished on top.

It never got down to a showdown over the coaches because the Reds cut it short by letting me go. I know for sure I was never gonna let the coaches leave before I did.

I can look the other way on a lot of different things. But don't test my loyalty. That can't be bought.

It wasn't the coaches' fault that we finished second two years in a row. We moved into first place in the first week of August and then the tornado hit. I had key guys going down with injuries like bowling pins. Injuries are a part of the game, but we started to look like a hospital ward.

Life has a funny way of evening things out. Sometimes our so-called failures are the direct result of another person's success. Let's don't be afraid to give credit where it's due. And then learn not to quit before getting it right the next time.

Tommy Lasorda did a great job for the Dodgers that year. He deserves to be in the Hall of Fame. I don't think any other manager—including me—could have gone into Los Angeles to follow Walter Alston and capture that city for 20 years like he did. The Dodgers won the pennant the first two years he was there. I always tease him that he's the guy who ran me out of the National League.

I don't care what kind of job you have. If you get fired, that's a kick to the head. It bruises your ego. After it happens, you must understand what went wrong. You can't sit and cry and feel sorry for yourself. You gotta get up, dust yourself off, and prove to everybody that if a mistake was made then you're gonna be a better person for it.

I remember the day I got fired from Cincinnati like it was yesterday. One of the reasons I was hit so hard was because I never saw it coming. When I met with Dick Wagner that day, I thought we were gonna talk about a couple of free agent players and clear up some other problems.

I'll say one thing . . . at least it was a short meeting.

We had breakfast in the coffee shop before going up to Dick's room—good old Number 1118. We got to the room and I flopped down in a big chair. Dick went into the bathroom for a couple of minutes.

When he came out, he walked up to me and said he had something very tough to tell me.

"We're not gonna bring you back," he said.

I'll never forget the words. At the time, though, they didn't really sink in. There were no harsh words from either side. He asked me some questions about some of the personnel like trainers and the traveling secretary. I gave him a good report on everybody. That's the way I felt about them.

When we were finished, I got up to leave. When I got to the door, Dick hugged me. He had tears in his eyes. I was pretty much in a daze all the time till I got home.

Until I told my family that Daddy just got fired, I had butterflies the size of bullfrogs inside my stomach. I felt like I had failed. After I got it out and they told me that they would love me no matter what happened, I got back in control again. I remember telling my young son, Albert, that we were gonna turn defeat into victory.

For the next three days I survived on coffee and soup. I got so tired I thought I was gonna pass out. I was either on the phone or doing some interview with a radio or television station.

The media made me out to be a bigger martyr than Joan of Arc. There was no time to get mad or sad or bitter or anything else, I was too busy. Besides, the next spring training was way too far off even to think anything had really changed.

After all the excitement started to die down, that's when reality started to sink in.

I have to admit that I wanted to prove the Reds wrong for firing me. I wanted to show them I could win without them. For about the next three years, I couldn't let that feeling go.

When the Tigers won in '84, I finally felt vindicated. It wasn't until years after that, though, before I released all the bitterness I never should have allowed to creep into my mind in the first place.

Getting fired ain't never no fun no matter what job you're doing. Jumping back up and taking control of your life, though, can make you a bigger person.

We all run into problems. It ain't how many pieces the picture breaks into. It's what you do with all the pieces to make it look right again.

When I look back at the Cincinnati situation, it was the best thing that ever happened to me. There were never no bad words from either side.

Some people wondered how The Big Red Machine could go on without me. I always said that Babe Ruth ain't around no more and they're still playing baseball.

The last time I looked, the Reds are still playing in the National League. And I wound up doing all right for myself.

I'll always remember Room 1118.

A Funny Thing Happened on the Way to Chicago

A funny thing happened on Sparky's way to becoming manager of the Chicago Cubs. He ran into Jim Campbell and wound up spending the next 17 years in Detroit.

For the most part, they were happy years. They comprised a run that may never again be seen in today's game. They also solidified Sparky's claim to an eventual berth in the Hall of Fame.

Campbell was the general manager of the Tigers and eventually became one of Sparky's closest friends. He was the primary reason why Sparky chose to manage the Tigers and remain there for the rest of his career.

A deal was only a signature away for Sparky to take over the Cubs after the 1979 season. After having been fired by the Reds, he decided to sit out a year for a couple of reasons. He was being paid by the Reds through the 1979 season. He also was doing promotions for Burger King and worked as a feature sports reporter for the ABC television station in Los Angeles.

More importantly, however, Sparky was confident he could return to baseball whenever he chose. In the first month after he was fired, he received six different offers to manage. Sparky decided not to come back until the 1980 season. He didn't want a club to fire a young manager just to hire him.

He listened to offers from the six interested clubs. At the time, the Tigers were not one of them.

Sparky was flattered by each. He picked the Cubs because he was impressed by General Manager Bob Kennedy.

Kennedy visited Sparky at his home in Thousand Oaks in early June. Sparky was particularly impressed by Kennedy's honesty and direct approach. Kennedy arranged for a meeting between Sparky and Cubs Owner Phil Wrigley whom Sparky had never met.

"But I chewed his gum since I was a kid," Sparky cracked.

At the time, Wrigley was at his estate on California's Catalina Island. The meeting occurred at a hotel in Ventura.

Sparky already had decided that a condition of his return would be a financially large contract with long-term security. He was confident about his managerial skills and did not wish to endure the disruptive dismissal process again. He wanted a five-year deal that included an insurance policy. The base salary was to start at $150,000 and rise each year according to the Consumers Index cost of living rate. Wrigley was comfortable with the terms. He had to check whether his company based cost of living on the Consumers Index before there could be a final agreement.

In Sparky's mind, the waiting was over. Starting the next spring, he would be manager of the Chicago Cubs.

Then along came Jim Campbell.

Sparky and Campbell had met several times in spring training when the Reds and Tigers played exhibitions. At the time Sparky was getting ready to go with the Cubs, the Tigers were playing a series in Anaheim. Sparky was at the game filming a pregame segment for his TV show.

The two encountered each other in the media lunchroom behind the press box prior to a game. Campbell introduced Sparky to Hall of Famer George Kell who was broadcasting the Tiger TV games. The three shared small talk and then went their own ways.

At the time, Don Drysdale was doing television for the Angels. Later that evening, Drysdale asked Sparky if he was going to manage again. Sparky told him that within the next ten days he was going to make a decision. It wouldn't take effect, however, until after the season.

Drysdale shared the information with Kell who then passed it along to Campbell. At about 11 o'clock the next morning, Sparky received a phone call from Campbell. It was a few days before the player trading deadline and Sparky thought Campbell wanted his impressions of a few players in the National League.

The conversation was brief and cordial. After a few minutes of small talk, almost abruptly, Campbell hung up.

A half hour later, Campbell called back. He was interested to know if Sparky was getting ready to make a decision about managing.

"Jim, you're a good person and I like you," Sparky told him. "With what I'm asking, you don't want no part of it."

At the time, the money Sparky was seeking set a precedent for managers.

"It's something to look at," Campbell casually replied after hearing the terms. Then as quickly as the last time, he hung up.

Campbell's comment had aroused Sparky's curiosity. He quickly thumbed through the Tiger media guide for a brief look at the players and their ages.

"I remembered from our spring training games that the Tigers had a young up-and-coming club," Sparky said. "There was never anything I enjoyed more than teaching young players and helping them to grow."

A half hour later, Campbell called again.

"Look, we'd like to get into this," he said. "You say you won't come till next year?"

Sparky answered "Absolutely not." Abruptly again, Campbell hung up.

Another half hour passed and again Campbell called. Campbell said the Tigers could wait the whole year and asked Sparky to think about it. By then Sparky knew the routine. Boom . . . Campbell hung up.

It took 30 minutes for Campbell to call again.

"I just can't do that," Campbell said. "There's no way I can look Les Moss (then Tiger manager) in the eye if I knew I was firing him at the end of the year. I never in my lifetime could do that."

Sparky appreciated Campbell's honest concern. But he also asked Campbell to understand that there was no way he was returning at the present time. Boom . . . Campbell hung up.

A half hour later, the phone rang again.

"What if I give you some time and then you come?" Campbell asked.

Again Sparky said no. One more time, boom . . . Campbell hung up.

Another half hour passed before the final call.

"Will you please come now?" Campbell asked.

"You're persistent," Sparky told him. "Anyone that persistent I've got to respect. Yes, I'll come now. But you've got to let me call all the other clubs who are interested so they don't read about this in the paper."

Sparky reached everybody. Ironically, the letter from the Cubs explaining that they did base their cost of living on the Consumers Index arrived the same day. Sparky thanked each interested club and told them he was going with the Tigers.

Two days later, Sparky was in Detroit. Seventeen years later, he still was there.

"You only get the chance to hire a Sparky Anderson once," Campbell explained. "We knew we had a good young team coming along. Sparky was the man who could take it to the top. He was the final piece of the puzzle.

"I had heard for many years what a good person he was in addition to his managerial skills. I just never realized how good. He actually became my best friend. I had a lot of managers in my career. Without a doubt, Sparky was the best."

Sparky's decision was based on more than Campbell's persistence. Through baseball's grapevine, he was well aware of Detroit's situation. Word within the game said that the Tigers were getting ready to blossom with some of baseball's brightest young talent.

Sparky also remembered a conversation he once had with former Tiger Manager Ralph Houk. Houk undertook a massive Tiger rebuilding project after a celebrated career with the Yankees.

"If you ever get a chance to work for Jim Campbell, take it," Houk told Sparky. "He's the best general manager in baseball and there's no better organization to work for than the Tigers."

Sparky had filed the tip in the back of his mind. When the opportunity presented itself, Sparky didn't let it slip away.

There are certain situations in every walk of life that seem to make a perfect connection. The Sparky/Tiger mix blended as beautifully as Casey Stengel with the Yankees.

Detroit certainly lacked the media glitz of New York. But Sparky provided a certain overwhelming presence that catapulted the Tigers into national prominence.

Even more important for Sparky, he had found a home in which he felt perfectly comfortable. He had always been a believer in baseball's simplistic purity. The Tigers were a throwback to the traditional fabric of baseball. Playing in quaintly historic Tiger Stadium, the Tigers remained a hallmark of always placing the game above all marketing gimmickry.

With the advent of player free agency, baseball had begun to turn to corporate style marketing methods to entice fans to the park. For the Tigers, effective marketing meant a competitive team on the field. In the seventeen years of Sparky's tenure, the Tigers finished under .500 only five times and all after the 1988 season.

In Detroit, there was a clearly defined chain of command. The manager was responsible solely to the general manager. The general manager was responsible to the owner alone. For Sparky, it was a throwback to the way he had been raised in the game.

"It's the way the game was meant to operate," Sparky said. "I'm not sure how much of that is still around today."

Even before Sparky's arrival, Campbell had never interfered with a manager's freedom to run the team. With Sparky, he felt even more comfortable than with any of the managers that had ever served under him.

"Sparky knew the game and lived it 24 hours a day," Campbell said. "He also was a man who knew how to run a team as men. You never saw any trouble with Sparky's teams. There were never any incidents in the clubhouse like you see with other teams. If we ran into a player that didn't fit, he didn't waste any time getting rid of him. He never let a bad apple spoil the rest of the bunch. There wasn't a player that put on that uniform who didn't know that Sparky was the boss."

Sparky played a hunch in 1979. The move turned into a 17-year run. The final curtain didn't fall until after the 1995 season. The longest managerial tenure in Tiger history included another World Championship, making Sparky the only manager ever to win a World Series in both leagues. He also established the Detroit franchise record of 1,331 victories.

The Cubs' loss almost two decades prior resulted in Detroit's biggest win since the invention of the assembly line.

And still loyal Cubs' fans can only wonder what might have been.

A Lesson in Loyalty

I made a mistake after the 1992 season when I stayed on with the Tigers.

When the team got sold, Jim Campbell and Bo Schembechler got fired. That's when I should have listened to my heart. I should have left with them.

I've always felt guilty that I stuck around after what happened to them. I have always maintained that when the people who were so close to you were ever mistreated, you go with them.

At the beginning of this book, I promised to all of you I would never tell a lie. I truly believe the only reason I stayed with the Tigers was because I fell into the trap I told all you young people never to do.

I allowed my high salary to keep me there. For that, I am probably more ashamed of myself than for anything I have ever done in baseball.

Jim Campbell and Bo Schembechler deserved more from me. Two people of that quality deserved for me to walk with them. I hope that none of you young people ever make the mistake I did.

Never let a pile of money dirty up that path between friends. Always honor your friends.

I should have left. I really didn't have a job no more, anyway. It was totally different.

Before I say anything about the Tigers, though, I want to say something about the Tiger fans.

For all the years I was blessed to be there, I never saw nothing like how those Tiger fans were. Those people were the real deal. Detroit is the king of the working class people. How can you not love a city where the fans sweat hard for eight hours a day and then come out to scream for their team and die a little bit every time the Tigers lost?

Sure, I wanted to win for myself. But I wanted to win as much for those fans as anybody else. They supported the Tigers. They supported the players. They supported me. I can't say nothing but thank you for all those wonderful times.

I wasn't even thinking about the Tigers when I got that first call from Campbell. And I wouldn't have given them a second thought if it hadn't been for that man.

Jim was a tough old baseball buzzard. He taught me more about life than anything about baseball. He was honest. He was loyal. He truly cared about his friends. You couldn't be around that man and not learn what all those qualities mean.

If there are any more important qualities in life than those, then I have no idea what they are.

Jim must have written that old kid's poem about sticks and stones breaking your bones but names never hurting you. He taught me that as long as you do the right thing and do it honestly . . . never to worry about what anybody else says.

That's a tough thing to do in baseball when the press starts sending those rockets at you. Sometimes they send them off without even knowing all the facts. But if you believe in what you're doing, and if you know what you're doing is the right thing, then you've got to keep walking a straight line and not worry about all the explosions that are going on around you. Jim was the best at that. He taught me how to stay the course.

I wish every young person would learn that lesson early in life. Don't waste a minute worrying about what somebody else is thinking. As long as you do the right thing, who cares what they say?

How's that gonna hurt you? If you know you're right, then you don't have to answer to nobody but yourself.

I think kids fall into that trap of doing what everybody else is doing when it comes to fooling around with drugs or drinking alcohol. They ain't purposely trying to break no rules. A lot of those kids do it because they're just too afraid to stand up and think for themselves.

It takes courage to walk alone. But every step you take along the right path makes you a bigger person. It don't matter what anybody else says.

Jim Campbell wasn't afraid of nothing or nobody. He was one of the most honest and loyal men I've ever been around.

If he shook your hand on something, you could go to the bank with it. You didn't need no contract. A lot of lawyers are funny people. Some of them know how to draw up a contract and some of them know how to get around one that was supposed to last forever.

I never saw a contract yet that was stronger than Jim Campbell's word. Once he gave you his word, that was a done deal. The Supreme Court couldn't break it. I learned that with the first Detroit contract I ever signed.

When I got to the ball park that first day, I must have spent about two hours with the press and all the radio and TV people before I even got a chance to see Jim. When I finally got up to his office, he was sitting there with a club lawyer.

Jim handed me the contract and told me to read it. He said if I wanted, I could have my lawyer read it before I signed.

"Is everything we talked about in this contract?" I asked him.

He said yes.

"Then give me a pen," I told him.

The lawyer asked if maybe I wanted him to read it to me. He was just doing his job.

"If that man there said everything is here, then I'm signing," I told him.

Jim never forgot that.

There was a similar incident that stayed close to his heart. It happened in 1988 when I was managing an All-Star team in Japan after the season. Carol and I were sleeping when the phone rang at about four in the morning.

"What's going on, big guy?" Jim said from back in Detroit.

"I'll tell you what's going on," I told him. "I'm sleeping, for crying out loud."

I knew something was bothering him. He had forgotten all about the time difference.

Jim said he had received a call that day from the California Angels. Gene Autry who owned the Angels owner asked for permission to talk to me about making a switch.

I listened to everything Jim had to say.

"Do you remember what I told you a couple of years ago?" I asked him when he was done.

"Didn't I tell you I'd never leave Detroit till you told me to go home to Thousand Oaks? And didn't you tell me that if that day ever came, you'd come out in a couple of weeks to play some golf with me? Now you please call Mr. Autry and tell him thank you. But I ain't going nowhere except back to sleep."

"You mean you don't even want to listen to them?" Jim asked.

"No, because if I do, I might find out how bad you been treating this little country boy for all these years," I joked.

Jim called the next night. He was almost crying. He said he'd told Tom Monaghan (Tiger owner) what I'd said. He said Monaghan couldn't believe I'd passed up more money and the chance to manage at home.

"I'll never forget this," Jim said.

Believe me . . . he never did.

If loyalty can be bought and sold like bread over the counter, then you'll never find me shopping at that market.

I loved my stay with the Tigers. Right up till the last couple of years, I got to know everybody and a little something about all of them.

Every day I used to walk through the offices and say hello to everybody. I knew every secretary and janitor and anybody else who worked there.

I never could understand how bosses in any kind of business can walk into the office with their head down. They don't want to look at people and at least say good morning. I honestly believe if people would just take the time to get to know who they're working with they'd be a lot happier.

I even got to know all the people who worked the concession stands at the park. After I made my visit to the front office every day, I used to walk under the stands and joke around with the ladies and all the old-timers who had been there for years.

People never read about these guys in the papers. They were just as important to me as the guy I had in left field that night. All they wanted was a little respect. Is that so hard to give to people?

That's the way the Tigers were under Jim Campbell and John Fetzer and Tom Monaghan. It was like a family. There were times when all of us might get angry with each other. But we'd work it out because we were all shooting for the same goal. We all knew where everybody stood all the time. There was never no second-guessing and talking behind each other's back.

With Jim, it was all baseball. He had everybody pushing in the same direction. That's the same way it was when Bo came over as president.

Forget all that stuff about Bo not being a "baseball man." Bo understands sports. More important than that, Bo knows people. He knows how to treat people and how to get the most out of them.

I used to watch Bo when he didn't even know I was looking. He used to do the same things I did. He didn't just talk to Alan Trammell or Lou Whitaker or Cecil Fielder. Bo would say hi to the guys on the grounds crew or the ladies selling hot dogs under the stands.

If you show people that you notice them and that you care, I guarantee you they'll show you how much they appreciate it.

If Bo Schembechler would have had the chance to stick around with the Tigers for a while, you would have seen one of the greatest executives that the Detroit franchise ever knew.

Bo was a great organizer. He was a tremendous communicator. He knew when to let people know that he wasn't satisfied with the job they were doing and he wasn't afraid to let people know when they were doing a good job.

I've seen so many bosses who are quick to criticize, but walk in quicksand when they should pat a guy on the back. Bo was so confident about himself that he wasn't afraid to do either one. That's the sign of a real leader.

Bo was only with the Tigers for two years, but he renovated that whole spring training complex and improved all the minor league facilities. As long as you showed him it was gonna help the organization, you could get anything you wanted from Bo.

If you had a problem, Bo felt it was his problem, too. It didn't matter where you were, he was there the next day.

That's the kind of leaders I worked for in Detroit. They taught me so many lessons I'll never be able to repay.

Even during the rough years at the end, I never second-guessed myself for going with the Tigers in the first place. It was a real family there. I don't know if baseball will ever have something like that again.

Nobody could have been treated better than I was. And nobody could have had better support from the fans like we did then.

Opportunity and Youth

Like so much of life according to Sparky, opportunity in his world is better understood in reverse.

The way he figures, you'll miss 100% of the chances you don't take.

When Sparky sniffs opportunity, he jumps on the wagon before the wheels get a chance to roll. He got that chance in Detroit. And the first day he arrived, he wasted no time proving why he was Sparky.

At a packed press conference at the park, he predicted the Tigers would be in a World Series before his five-year contract was complete.

That's an eternity for hungry baseball fans. But with Detroit craving a Series appearance for the first time since 1968, the promise was welcomed like Ann-Margret on a Bob Hope goodwill military tour.

The Tigers, at the time, had one of the brightest collections of young talent sprinkled throughout their farm system. It was the eve of some of Detroit's most glorious history.

There was no quick fix, though. Only the chance to tinker with the tools.

That was good enough for Sparky. The challenge was there. He came to Detroit packing enthusiasm and promise, not a magic wand.

"If Sparky would have known what he knew after he had taken the job, he probably wouldn't have taken it," joked Alan Trammell. The long-time shortstop and his second base sidekick Lou Whitaker were only in their second full season with Detroit.

"He probably thought we were a little better prepared and had a little more talent than we actually did," Trammell continued.

Sparky never second-guessed his decision to go to Detroit. For him, the situation was perfect. He had returned to the game with a franchise steeped in tradition and with the opportunity to contribute to it. He could develop young players and teach them the wisdom of discipline.

Not only did he make good on his five-year deal, the Tigers wound up as one of the most winning franchises in either league for the decade of the '80s.

"It was the perfect situation for him," said Billy Consolo, who came with Sparky to Detroit as a coach. "We had all these good young prospects like Alan Trammell and Lou Whitaker and Kirk Gibson and Lance Parrish and Jack Morris and Dan Petry. There's nothing Sparky loves to do more than teach.

"I remember going to the big leagues when I was eighteen years old. A new manager would come in and say, 'You guys are major leaguers . . . we teach in the minors.'

"That's not Sparky. He loves to teach baseball. He'd have those kids out there at two o'clock in the afternoon for instructions before a night game. He loves helping young people develop on the field and off."

Some of the talent Sparky had inherited was as raw as a broken blister. They had to learn how to play together. More importantly to Sparky, they needed a crash course in how to conduct themselves as professionals.

"Early in my career we were playing a series in Baltimore," recalled Kirk Gibson. "At that time, the Orioles always had a fundamentally sound club. They'd do some little thing in the field to stop a rally and Sparky would say, 'Now see . . . that's what I'm talking about.' He'd have all of us out early the next day practicing what we'd seen the previous night. He drilled us. That's how he molded us into world champions."

There was purpose for that drilling. It established a system of discipline.

Sparky got an opportunity to teach the youngsters and

the World Champions in-waiting received an intangible in return.

Sparky brought a presence few other managers enjoy. His stature not only permeated the whole Tiger organization, it also was embraced by the entire American League. He already had been hailed as one of the most celebrated ambassadors of the game.

The Tigers finally had a legitimate piece of national sports notoriety. Everyone knew Sparky. He was just as determined for everyone to appreciate his young team.

"I'm somewhat of a baseball historian," Trammell said. "So when he came to Detroit, I was in awe of him. I knew what he had done at Cincinnati. When he came, he got all of our attention.

"He was exactly what we needed. We needed to be corralled. We needed direction. We hadn't yet learned how to act as major leaguers. He was the guy who got us going."

Even to this day, Trammell marvels at the attention that follows Sparky wherever he goes.

"When Sparky Anderson walks into a room, he immediately grabs your attention," Trammell said. "You know he's in charge. We needed that.

"He was sort of like a high school principal. You always looked out of the corner of your eye to see if he was watching because he always seemed to be there. It always made you act properly. You wanted to do the right things. After we developed, he gave us a little rope. He not only wanted to teach us how to play on the field, but also how to conduct ourselves professionally away from the park."

When Sparky first went to Cincinnati, the Reds were more advanced than the Tigers he inherited in 1979. The character development program was triggered into action at Detroit just as it had been done at Cincinnati a decade earlier.

Sparky always believed that a player's skills defined only half of the individual. If his young men never became responsible citizens, they were nothing more than ball players.

So Sparky went about his business of baseball and character building. Sometimes the latter was the toughest part of the job.

"He was a man who would rather surround himself with good quality people than just somebody who could play baseball well," Parrish said. "I knew that just by the friends of his that I met.

"He was up-front about not wasting his time having bad people in the clubhouse. It was important to have a talented ball club, but it was just as important to him to have quality people. I always admired that. He would never let an individual come along and embarrass the club or baseball."

Gibson still chuckles when he fondly remembers Sparky's "weed and garden speech."

"He used to say, 'I like my vegetables to grow good. If there's a weed in there, I'm gonna take it out.'

"That was his way of saying if you're a jerk, you're out of here. He took the time to show us how he wanted things done. If you didn't conform, you were gone. He had a direction. You knew what it was and if you didn't follow it, he had no use for you. And he was right. That's the way it should be. Not just in baseball, but for every part of our society."

Gibson turned out to be one of Sparky's all-time pet projects. The two didn't particularly mesh the first three-and-a-half years of Gibson's Tiger career.

When Gibson burst onto the scene, Sparky tagged him as the next Mickey Mantle. Later Sparky was sorry he put such pressure on his prize pupil.

Gibson struggled. Not only with the burden of such high expectations, but also with his battle of learning how to become the professional person Sparky so much wanted him to be.

"When I first came up, I wasn't focused on what I was there for," Gibson admitted. "He didn't like what he saw in me as a person. He sat me down and gave me a good talking to. He said he'd seen a lot of good talent go wasted. His interest was for me as a person. He wanted me to learn the game of baseball and learn how to treat people right.

"It took four to five years to get through to me. With his help, though, I conquered the beast. He's a guy who really wants to give back to others. He feels he owes something to the game."

Sparky was fearless in calling all the shots. Still, he kept an open door policy to his office. Players were always welcome to express their concerns. Sparky would listen, then pass judgment based on doing the right thing.

He used the democratic three-vote system. The player had one vote and Sparky had two.

Gibson spent a lot of time in Sparky's office. Both enjoyed the mental duels that only a couple of driven personalities could share.

One pregame meeting in Yankee Stadium particularly impressed Sparky. With the hard-throwing left-handed Ron Guidry scheduled to start for the Yankees, Sparky did not have the left-handed hitting Gibson in the starting lineup. Shortly before game time, Tiger center fielder Chet Lemon became ill and was unable to start. Gibson was summoned to Sparky's office.

"Would it bother you if you had to play against Guidry?" Sparky asked.

"No," Gibson simply barked.

Thirty-seconds later a hostile Gibson charged back into the office.

"I'm going to tell you something and listen to me carefully," Gibson growled. "Don't ever embarrass me again wondering if I can play against anybody. You put my name in the lineup and I play."

No one appreciated that type of competitiveness more than Sparky. He never possessed the physical talent Gibson did. Both were kindred spirits, though, in fighting uphill battles all their lives.

"He's like a father to me," Gibson said. "We challenged each other. We pushed each other for the good of ourselves."

Gibson actually regaled in his role of self-proclaimed ornery prince of nastiness. Once in a while he had to share the spotlight with all-time Tiger winner Jack Morris.

At times, the right-hander could be as nasty off the mound as his split-finger fastball was on it.

Sparky appreciated Morris' brand of nastiness. He

likened him to a thoroughbred that got a little more ornery as each minute ticked off before a big race. Sparky's office often was the site of heated discussions between the two.

"The greatest thing about Sparky is that I realized he was my boss and that I was one of the role players on the team," Morris said. "He established that.

"But we could still communicate. Sparky always felt the door was open if the boys wanted to talk. There were times when we had to get things off our chests. I think that was one of the best things about our relationship . . . the fact that we didn't always agree, but we agreed to disagree and then go about our business."

Morris' business was about being one of the most intimidating pitchers of the '80s. For over a period of years, he was, by far, the best pitcher Sparky ever managed.

Morris went on to pitch for two other World Championship teams—the Minnesota Twins and Toronto Blue Jays—after his Detroit career.

"How can I say anything but that Sparky was the best," Morris said. "He gave me the ball. He gave me the opportunity that some other managers wouldn't have. He taught me how to pitch by keeping me in there to rot. I had to pitch my way out of a lot of crap. I don't look at that as a negative thing. It was very positive. At a young age I was taught what it meant to finish a game. Learning to finish what you start is one of the greatest lessons any young person can receive."

So in spite of some stormy sessions between wizened manager and rambunctious young pitcher, Morris appreciates the influence Sparky had on his career and character.

"My parents taught me this, but it was Sparky who reminded me all the time," Morris said. "He always stressed treating people the way you want to be treated. The easiest thing to do is find fault in another. The hardest is to find some good in people who are having tough times."

The Tigers made an unexpected pennant run in the strike-shortened split season of 1981. In 1983, the young crop of bright Tiger prospects proved they were on the brink of stardom by winning 92 games and finishing second.

The magical season of 1984 saw the Tigers lead wire-to-wire. They captured their first World Championship since 1968 to make good on Sparky's five-year deal.

In 1987, the Tigers overcame overwhelming odds to win the American League East title in what Sparky calls his most satisfying season. With eight games to play, the Tigers rallied from a 3 1/2 game deficit to beat Toronto by two games.

When Sparky finally finished his Detroit career after the 1995 season, he walked away as the most winning manager in franchise history with 1,331 victories. Hughie Jennings is second with 1,131.

"What you have to remember about Sparky more than anything else is that he's an old-time baseball guy," Trammell said. "He's from the old school and I say that very complimentary. I think that today there's still some things from the old school that need to be taught.

"One of the most important is to treat people the way you want to be treated. He's a big-name star. On the inside, though, he's just a straightforward street guy with a tremendous work ethic. I love him."

A Character Check

You can win a few battles with people who lack character. I'll damn sure guarantee you, though, you won't win no war.

I don't care if it's a ball player or the guy who sweeps up the park after the games. Success don't come till a person develops character inside and out.

I ain't no dummy. I knew the kind of baseball talent I was getting when I went to Detroit. Howdy Doody could have seen all those good young players in their organization.

What they had to learn before they became champions is what a champion is really made of.

If the core ain't healthy, that apple is gonna rot. All the talent in the world can't make up for a lack of character. That goes for ball players, priests, business leaders and all the people who punch a clock.

It's impossible to reach your goals on the outside if your insides ain't strong enough to grind it out when the going gets tough.

When I got to Detroit I wasn't sure what I'd say to the press. That five-year deal just sorta popped into my head.

I knew the raw material was there. I was confident in myself and in my coaches that we could mold them in that time. If I didn't, I wouldn't be around anyway because then I deserved to be fired.

Anyway, the five-year plan gave the boys in the press something to write about.

What I didn't know when I got there was that it would take the full five years. Those kids had talent. But they were rougher than a three-day beard.

The first thing I had to do was establish direction. Those kids were like a bunch of wild stallions. I knew once they were broken they could run till the sun went down. Talent without discipline, though, is like lemonade without the lemon.

I don't care if a youngster is in school or he's starting his first job. Even if they don't show it, all kids want to be disciplined.

They want to be taught the right way to do things. Shame on us old-timers if we don't take the time to provide that direction.

Those young Tigers had all the physical tools. But we had to teach fundamentals till they could do them in their sleep.

We had sessions before the games. And everybody had to be on time. We worked on bunting. We drilled the hit-and-run. We made the cutoff play a friend instead of an enemy. If we got beat, it wasn't gonna be because we were a bunch of alley players.

And they weren't gonna become professionals on the field till they learned how to conduct themselves before they even showed up at the park.

I couldn't believe the first road trip we took. Those guys didn't look like a major league team going on an airplane to represent Detroit. They showed up wearing Levis and sweatshirts and sneakers.

I asked one of my coaches if we were going to the rodeo.

Coats and ties were required for the next trip. Alcoholic drinks were barred from all flights.

What you bring to your job, you carry right on to your job. If you're lazy, you're going to be lazy at your work. If you're a slob, you'll be sloppy on the job, too.

If you carry yourself proudly, you look like a pro.

Even if you don't win, at least you give yourself a chance.

We were blessed with a lot of good young men. They took to the program quickly. They wanted to be disciplined. Those that didn't, weren't around for too long.

For pure talent, Alan Trammell, Lou Whitaker, Lance Parrish, and Kirk Gibson could put on a clinic. I don't want to slight any of our other players. But I don't know of any other team in those years that had four players any better on their club than those guys.

Trammell was the textbook player for all young people to follow. Not just young ball players. I mean any young person who wants to learn how to get the most out of their talent whatever it might be.

Trammell had talent. But not as much as the star he turned out to be. He did it by hard work. He simply refused to quit. He took extra ground balls at short. He took batting practice till his hands bled. He studied the moves of every opposing player. And he wasn't afraid to ask questions.

He fielded every ball hit his way the most proper way you're supposed to. And that's all because of discipline.

He knew he didn't have the arm that some shortstops are blessed with. So he learned every hitter in the league so that he could place himself in the right position. He forced himself to do everything properly to make up for any physical skills he might not have had. He was always prepared.

Whitaker was different. He had so much talent. He couldn't hide it even if he played under a blanket.

Lou was a street player. He played by feel. He played totally on his God-given abilities and didn't go by no book. He never played his position based on scouting reports on the hitters.

Nobody had softer hands. He could have been a pickpocket. He got his share of bad hops, but nobody never noticed because he was so quick.

Lou got with the program in his own way. He was quiet as a whisper and never caused no problems. When he showed up for a road trip, he was dressed like he was going to the prom. He looked like a big leaguer and he played like one.

Trammell and Whitaker were like peanut butter and jelly. You couldn't think of one without the other. Detroit will never see another pair like that again.

Parrish is a very special person in my career. When he first came up, he never said a sentence with more than two words. And then you had to strain your ears to hear what he was saying.

By the time we were ready to win, he had developed into the unofficial leader of the team.

Being the catcher, Lance had to learn how to take charge. When he did, the other players looked up to him.

I was so proud of the way Lance learned to handle the media. When he talked, everybody listened. I never had to worry about what he would say. He had matured. He realized his own role and also the role of the media.

We stressed that everybody had his own role to fill. We can all accomplish a lot more if we cooperate with those around us. Lance disciplined himself to accept that role. He's one of my all-time favorites to have been around day after day.

Gibson was a totally different animal. He probably was the toughest project I had in my career.

For pure physical talent, Gibby needed two empty boxcars to haul it to the park every day. The only thing he had more of than talent was a severe case of meanness that snapped at everyone in his way.

I respected that meanness. It drove Gibby past all the limits where other players feared to walk. But he had to learn to harness that drive. He had to learn how to treat people the way he expected to be treated.

By the time he left Detroit, Gibby was a human being. He never wanted to be bothered when he was going about his business. Finally, though, he came to accept that Kirk Gibson was not the only person on the face of the earth.

I ain't ashamed to say that I love Kirk Gibson. I love the way he wasn't afraid to admit he had to mature. And I love the way he put the team ahead of any personal agenda.

Half of Gibby's game plan was to intimidate the opposition. He dared anyone to step in his way. When he had his mind set on something, he wanted someone to try to stop him.

He was the ultimate team player. When he went 3-for-4 and we lost, he could bite off the head of a rattlesnake. When he went 0-for-4 and we won, he ran around the clubhouse like he had hit two grand slams and stole the mustard off somebody's hot dog.

Gibby will probably never go into the Hall of Fame. But he was a Hall of Fame performer. He hit more game-winning home runs than anyone I ever saw in my career.

Gibby was a true winner. He's the perfect team player.

Whatever you do for a living, you'll get a lot more done if you put your team's goals ahead of your own.

If Gibby learned anything from me, I'm grateful. I'm glad I had the chance to manage him because he gave me so much pleasure. Probably more than I gave him.

Jack Morris had his own kind of ugly. He had the stubbornness of a mule and the grace of a thoroughbred.

When we absolutely had to win a game, I wanted Morris on the mound over any pitcher you'd give me. Nine out of ten times he'd win. The other time he'd keep you close enough for a shot at the end.

Jack is a perfect lesson in determination. It's so easy

in life to give up when the going gets rocky. That's when Morris really got going.

Once he started a game, it took an act of Congress to get him out. Jack was a great believer in always finishing what he started. Quitters want to bail when the arrows start flying. Jack stared at those arrows and dared them to come his way.

I respect anyone who ain't afraid to stand in the middle of the ring when all the punches are coming from the other direction. He's the best pitcher I ever had. And one of the toughest competitors.

As much as I taught all those guys on the Tigers, I think they taught me at least as much. They showed me how much youngsters really want to make out of their lives. And when they become disciplined, there's no limit to what they can do.

The Perfect Summer?

Sparky's five-year promise of making it to the World Series was kept. But not even Sparky thought it would happen the way it did.

The 1984 season gave Detroit seven months of New Year's Eve. It started on the first day of the season and didn't stop until October 14th.

The Tigers clinched their first World Championship in 16 years. The happy conclusion may not have been as delirious as the way they arrived.

The Tigers started the season with a nine-game winning streak and led the American League East Division wire-to-wire. They set a franchise attendance record of 2,704,794 and the fans partied all year long.

The Tigers swept three straight games from Kansas City in the Playoffs. They rolled over San Diego in five games in the World Series.

For ecstatic Tiger fans, they were deliciously sweet times. For Sparky, it was hell.

The experience was similar to military service. When the tour of duty is finished, you're grateful for the experience. While that service meter is running, though, the days crawl by like turtles.

"We got out of the gate so fast, we outran our shadow," Sparky said. "That was fine. But I felt pressure like I never felt before. We built such a big lead early that all the experts had us winning the World Series by Father's Day.

"I know what can happen during a season. Slumps. Injuries. All kinds of freak things. Now if that happens and we don't win, there's only one scalp everyone's hunting for.

That's the manager's because he ain't supposed to let those things happen."

Even in that magical year, there were slumps. And there were a few minor injuries.

Not even Harry Houdini could have tricked the Tigers out of winning that year. They had finally matured into a collection of disciplined young professionals.

The Tigers weren't destined to win. Destiny smiles only on those more determined than the opposition to shape the final outcome. Detroit won because no team on the planet was more determined than the 1984 Tigers. They set a major league record by winning 35 of their first 40 games and never looked back.

"We were a bunch of guys with no names," Jack Morris recalled. "In all honesty, we didn't have any superstars. We had a lot of guys that contributed and no one would recognize them now. We were a winning team. We weren't that much physically better than anyone else. We were mentally tough."

Most of the headlines went to guys like Morris and Gibson and Trammell and Whitaker and Parrish and Hernandez. Victory, though, was the result of a whole roster playing together all season. Each member contributed in his own special way.

"It was the epitome of the team concept," said first baseman and pinch hitter deluxe Dave Bergman.

"Everybody came to the yard ready to play every day. I remember games when the other team started a left-hander and then brought in a righty as early as the second inning. Sparky wasn't afraid to put a whole new team in the lineup. We all got a chance to contribute."

Bergman was traded to the Tigers shortly before the end of spring training in 1984. In December, the Tigers had signed free agent Darrell Evans to play first base. Bergman understood he would not be a starter. He accepted his role. He was the model of Sparky's perfect player. He was physically and mentally tough and always prepared to play.

"That's the way Sparky molded his team," Bergman said. "One or two guys can't carry a team for a whole season. But a whole team can carry one or two guys when they're in a slump.

"It's the same principle for any successful business. No one person is bigger than the company. When everybody strives for a common goal, the company generally works for all the individuals."

Today Bergman is a successful financial planner in the Detroit area. He credits much of his business success to his experience under Sparky.

Bergman also understood the intricacies of the game as well as any coach.

"When I came to Detroit, I was fairly knowledgeable as far as the game was concerned," he said. "My basic fundamentals were pretty sharp.

"I can't honestly say that Sparky taught me that much about the game. What he taught me was how to be a man. To me, that was more important than anything he could have taught me about baseball.

"He taught me to be honest and straightforward with people. Sometimes my honesty gets me into trouble. But it's much easier for me to remember the truth instead of a pack of lies."

The regular starters that year understood the merits of Sparky's liberal system of using all his players.

"You never knew when he was going to call on somebody at any point of the game," said Alan Trammell. "He was so sharp that he knew a certain player in just the right situation could mean the difference in a game. It didn't matter if it was early in a game or late, everybody better be ready. That kept everybody sharp. When the Playoffs and World Series rolled around, everybody was at their peak. Nobody was tired."

After playing ball with Sparky since the time they were twelve years old and then coaching for his friend for five years, Billy Consolo thought he knew everything about the way Sparky went about running a team.

"Sometimes he posted a lineup that would absolutely shock the coaches," Consolo said. "He put somebody in the lineup that we'd never dream of. And then the guy would come through."

Rusty Kuntz was a perfect example. For the previous five years he bounced around several teams struggling to stay in the big leagues. In 1984, he played in a career-high 84 games and somehow managed to come up with several clutch hits. He actually scored the winning run in the final game of the World Series.

"Sparky would just have feelings," Consolo said. "He kept everyone ready to play. He was never afraid to use all of his people. He amazed me.

"In the old days when I played, the manager had the same eight guys in the lineup every day. You didn't come on one of Sparky's teams and think you were going to sit around for four hours."

Sparky's five-year plan of making it to the World Series checked in just on time. Once the Tigers made it to the Series, no one was going to let the ride would stop there.

History's most meteoric start kept the Tigers in front throughout the season. By the time they ran their record to 35–5 on May 24th, they had built a comfortable 8 1/2 game lead. They stretched it to 10 by the end of June and 12 1/2 at the end of July. It never dipped below 7 1/2 games. They won the East Division by 15 games over Toronto.

Nevertheless, Sparky worried incessantly about a letdown. He felt he and his team had something to prove. They wanted no prisoners. They were dead set on destruction.

Before the World Series, Sparky was outraged by a scouting report the San Diego Padres had prepared on his Tigers. Sparky, his coaches, General Manager Bill Lajoie and the Tiger scouts had a meeting before the Series. At the meeting, they dissected each player on the Padres. Sparky also was informed that the Padres believed that the Tigers couldn't run.

Sparky became consumed by the challenge. It provided an opportunity to exploit just one more team's miscalculation.

"When Sparky held a meeting with the players, he took this report and set it down by his side," Consolo laughed. "He looked at those kids and said 'Boys, we're running. We're gonna hit-and-run . . . we're gonna steal . . . we're gonna do everything in this World Series.' And we did.

"I don't think Darrell Evans had stolen a base in ten years. The first time he got on, Sparky put on a hit-and-run play. He was telling the Padres—whatever you got on us, we're going after you. When I saw Evans taking off from first base, I said to myself, 'Sparky's going after the whole shebang.'"

He did. And the Padres got shebunged in just five games. The clincher came in Detroit on Sunday evening. Gibson hammered a pair of home runs in an 8–4 clincher that sent the whole state of Michigan into a frenzy.

"I think that scouting report got under Sparky's skin," Trammell said. "The way we attacked the Padres was a very important part of the Series.

"Right from the get-go we played some hit-and-run and did some things to put a little pressure on them. We wanted to tell them—hey, we're not going to just sit back and wait. We jumped on them quick. Not just by running, but by moving up runners and doing a lot of little things. I think we caught them by surprise."

Only the Padres must have felt that way. The rest of the country expected nothing less than total domination by Detroit. In fact, by the time the Series came around, almost everyone had conceded the crown to Detroit.

Everybody but Sparky, that is. For him, it was a struggle right to the moment when left fielder Larry Herndon squeezed his glove around the last out of the ninth inning in Game Five.

The season of ecstasy and torment was finally over. Sparky had become the only manager in history to win a World Series in both leagues.

Now he had to try to recover from being torn somewhere between heaven and hell.

A Very Painful Wake-Up

I thought about retiring after we won the 1984 Series.

I was surprised that would even enter my mind. It lasted for only a little while, but it was there.

Roger Craig was my pitching coach. He was one of the best I ever saw my whole career. He told me near the end of the season that, win or lose, he was gonna retire after the year.

After we won the whole thing, he said, "Come on. Let's go out together. You won in both leagues now. You can't do no more."

I thought about it. For maybe three weeks, it ran through my mind a lot. But after I was home for a while and all of the hoopla got out of my system, I knew I had to come back. I had to give all the other managers another shot at me.

I know how much that World Series meant to Detroit. I'm happy for the organization and all those people in Michigan who got so much pleasure out of it.

I was pleased to see how those young men had matured. They won because they had developed as men even more than they had as players.

I have to admit, though, it was a terrible year for me. I'm sorry to say it's one I'd like to forget. I don't regard it as one of my nicest years.

The team played super. And I'm not ashamed to say that I did a pretty good job of managing. But I ain't happy with the way I handled myself all the way up till we won the thing.

I did so many things wrong. That's why I'd like to be able to relive that year.

For five years before that, I lived with that beast of wanting to show the Reds what a big mistake they had made by firing me. When I got fired, I did all the right things. I said all the right things. Inside, though, my stomach never stopped burning.

Now how dumb can one man be?

I wanted to show Cincinnati up. Now isn't that a wonderful thing to do? What did we show? That we could beat San Diego in a World Series? That's all. Cincinnati didn't break down and quit playing baseball just because we beat the Padres.

I had such a madness about me to win the World Series. I went way beyond all the boundaries. Nobody should be obsessed with anything that bad. Nobody should be so obsessed with their ego that they feel like their life depended on winning something in baseball.

If I could apologize, I would. But who do I apologize to? The only person I can apologize to is myself for acting like that. I'm the one who went through it. I'm the one who suffered.

I remember walking back and forth in my kitchen after games all summer long. I kept telling my wife, "I gotta win . . . I gotta win . . . I gotta win."

Gotta win what? I let the ego jump in and take over total control. I thought I had to win so that nobody could question me after winning in both leagues. Then I could never be accused again that I could only win in Cincinnati.

I knew I had to go back to all the things Lefty Phillips had taught me. It was all right to attack as hard as I could. But then I had to let things go.

I allowed myself to become so consumed about being the first person to do something like win in both leagues. Whenever I hear that now, it don't even concern me.

It don't concern me because now I realize that wasn't the reason I went into baseball in the first place. I went into baseball because I love the game. I always wanted to do whatever it took to make the game better and help young players. I never worried about my own success.

That 1984 season taught me a great lesson.

When I talk to young people, I talk straight from the heart. Ol' Sparky was stupid to get so consumed over something like that. Don't do something stupid like him.

Whether you're a real estate person, a doctor, a lawyer, an insurance agent, a plumber, an electrician, a truck driver, it doesn't matter. You are not in any business except to do the very best you can do at that job.

It's all right to set goals. It's all right to push yourself to the limit. Just don't push yourself over the edge. Dedication and obsession are two different things. I crossed the line and made that summer miserable for myself.

Do your best then leave it alone. There ain't nothing more you can do. Don't trip on your ego trip on the way to the bank.

There ain't a day that goes by that I ain't reminded about how dumb I was. Just read the paper or watch TV and see how many people lose their loved ones or how many families are devastated by some crippling disease.

If you think you've got problems, just take a look around. Winning that season opened my eyes a lot.

The whole season was strange because so many good things happened so fast. We started 35–5 and were actually in all the games we lost.

Cal Ripken, Jr. proved a couple of years ago that no record is untouchable. I just don't see how any team will ever again start the season by winning 35 of their first 40 games.

When you start 35–5, you have to win. Every time a visiting manager came to Detroit after that, I told them to take a look at that flag pole in center field. If we don't win, there's only gonna be one person hanging from it. It ain't gonna be no players. It ain't gonna be no coaches. It ain't gonna be the general manager and it sure ain't gonna be the owner.

The only person hanging from that pole if we didn't win was gonna be little ol' Sparky.

When you jump off to a start like that, everybody declares you the winner by Memorial Day. That includes all the fans, all the writers, and all the baseball people.

Well, what if you lose four guys to injuries? And that can easily happen. Now nobody ain't gonna say four guys got injured. They're gonna say this was the biggest fold job since Scrooge folded his wallet and stuck it in his back pocket.

And that's when the manager gets the blame.

I couldn't shake that feeling all season long. I probably felt more pressure that year than I did in '89 when we lost 103 games.

I remember in early August, we got swept by Kansas City in a four-game series in Detroit just before we had to go to Boston for a five-game series. The Red Sox had a pretty good team at the time.

I had some very dear friends in Boston. They always brought the family up when we came to town. They stayed in one room of my suite.

I remember getting to Boston Sunday night after losing a doubleheader. There was no way I could get to sleep. I walked back and forth between those two rooms till seven in the morning. I called up my friends and told them they better not come. I was too edgy. I didn't think I'd be a very nice host.

We took two of those five games in Boston while Toronto got swept in Texas. We went to Kansas City for another four-game series and swept the Royals. About three weeks later we went to Toronto and swept a three-game series. For the first time all season, I finally relaxed a little. I could tell for sure that this club had grown up.

We opened the Playoffs in Kansas City. After we won that first game, I knew we were headed to the Series. It was the same thing there. When we won that first game in San Diego, I knew nothing could stop us from finishing the job everybody but me thought we were gonna do.

Every player on that 1984 team did exactly what their role called for. If you ever watched a stage play where every actor played their part perfectly, that's the way our team performed.

Even the biggest stars on Broadway can't do their jobs without the good role players.

I don't think people realize how good that 1984 team really was. The '76 Reds was the best team I ever managed. Maybe the '75 team was second. That '84 club, though, was a solid third.

They had come a long way from their blue jeans and tee-shirts, wondering why they never won.

I wish I could look back and say that I enjoyed that season more than I did. Now I can only hope that all the young people will learn from my mistakes.

No matter what you do . . . give it your best shot and then let it alone. There ain't no job in this world that's so important to ever let your ego get in the way.

And When I'm Bad

When movie vixen Mae West purred something like "when I'm good I'm very good, but when I'm bad I'm better," she didn't exactly have baseball on her mind.

The sultry star and Sparky share as much in common as a pop to shortstop and a breakfast pop tart.

By mere coincidence, however, her immortal line captures part of the spirit of Sparky's fascination for baseball.

Maybe it's because of the length of the season. Maybe it's too much time on the road.

Whatever the reason, Sparky is convinced that no other sport concocts highs and lows quite as potent as does baseball.

"It's up and down . . . just like a runaway elevator," Sparky said. "And both are hundred-proof. There ain't no better feeling than one of those highs.

"Nobody wants to feel bad, so I know it sounds crazy. But after so many years in the game, you get addicted to the swing. You almost start looking for a low. I can't explain it. And those lows can make you shiver in summer."

In the space of two years, Sparky took the ultimate emotional baseball ride.

Nothing in Sparky's professional career matches the pride he feels for his 1987 team which almost snatched the American League pennant.

In 1989 he was ambushed by a pack of emotional demons. This low ripped savagely beyond baseball's normal range of mood swings. It actually threatened to end his colorful career.

Both seasons pushed the limits even within the norms of Sparky's quite abnormal life. Footprints and memories still linger from both.

In 1987, the Tigers weren't expected to do much more than finish their 162-game season on time. Most preseason polls picked them to finish somewhere in the middle of the American League's East Division. Chances of making it to post-season play were rated at about the same odds as Sparky's hair turning black.

In the season's last 11 days, the Tigers transformed into a real-life Lazarus. In one of baseball's most memorable seven-game sets with Toronto, the Tigers rose from the dead to make the Playoffs against Minnesota.

"No team ever made me feel prouder than that one," Sparky said. "I'm grateful for those World Series. But this was different. We didn't make it to the Series, but it still proved what people can do when they really believe in themselves and simply refuse to quit."

To this day, Sparky still can't explain how it happened.

"We were supposed to finish way down somewhere in South America according to all the experts," Sparky said. "But somehow that team pulled together. We had no business running with the big boys. It was pure determination."

In the winter of 1986, the Tigers lost free agent catcher Lance Parrish to the Philadelphia Phillies. Throughout 1987, Sparky maneuvered around a hodgepodge pitching staff. He tiptoed over a variety of injuries to key players.

The "Miracle of Michigan and Trumbull Avenues" earned him the American League Manager of the Year Award.

The season began as dismally as most experts had predicted. By May 5th, the Tigers had tumbled to last place, a whopping 11 games out of first.

It was at that point Sparky appeared once again to have shoved his spike down his well-worn throat. In the face of a disbelieving press, he boldly predicted that the Tigers would be in the race before the season was over. It took almost five months for the final skeptics to be silenced.

On the season's final day, the Tigers were the last team standing after their famous seven-game showdown with

Toronto that sent baseball historians scurrying through the record books.

"Sparky always gave us the same speech in spring training," Gibson recalled. "Whenever we left Florida, we believed we were going to become World Champions.

"But he knew in his heart that the '87 team didn't have that much talent. Of all the teams he ever managed, this one won on sheer heart and determination. We had guys like Tommy Brookens who was a tremendous overachiever. Tommy didn't have that much talent. Our whole team was like that."

Overachievement became the norm. For some unexplainable reason, they managed to snare that runaway rabbit when all the ammunition already had been spent.

Only Alan Trammell posted a career year. He finished second in the voting for the Most Valuable Player Award by hitting .343 with 28 home runs and 105 runs batted in. No other full-time player batted .300. None had 100 RBI. Jack Morris led the pitchers with an 18–11 won-lost record. Doyle Alexander, who joined the Tigers in an August 12th trade for minor leaguer John Smoltz, rejuvenated the staff by going 9–0.

"In 1984, we probably had the best club I played on in Detroit," Morris said. "In '87, we were less talented but typical overachievers.

"We didn't realize we weren't that good. We thought we were good and played that way. In all honesty, we probably didn't deserve to be in the Playoffs. But we persevered and beat Toronto.

"Sparky deserves a lot of the credit. As the manager, his attitude was portrayed by his players. A lot of people can say all a manager does is fill out the lineup card. That's true in a lot of cases. If you've got the horses, let them run. On the other hand, you've got to find out about all the role players and give them the opportunity to contribute. Sparky was a master that way."

Trammell led the team in games played with 151. Darrell Evans was the only other to appear in 150 games. Everybody else took turns at playing hero of the day. No one cared who grabbed the spotlight as long as the job got done.

A will to win consumed the entire team. Fancy numbers and statistics were left for the rest of the league.

"We had a closeness that put everything else aside," Gibson explained. "When we got to the white lines, we were totally one together. There was no conflict at all. Nothing. We didn't carry anything onto that field except togetherness.

"Sparky was good at preparing us for that. He regulated that. It goes back to his clubhouse. He knew that without distraction from the clubhouse during a game, we were much better off."

When the Tigers visited first place Toronto on the next to last Thursday of the season, they were tighter than a New York City subway on a late Friday afternoon.

The Tigers entered that four-game series trailing the Blue Jays by one-half game. The Tigers lost the first game, 4–3. They dropped the second, 3–2. They were outslugged in the third, 10–9, to fall 3 1/2 games back with only eight left to play.

On that Sunday afternoon in Toronto, the Blue Jays threatened to sweep the series when they took a 1–0 lead into the top of the ninth inning. In typical Gibson drama, he tied the game by leading off the ninth with a home run. He won it in the 13th with a run-scoring single.

After the game, Gibson took a page out of Sparky's own book of media relations. Gibson's daring comments made headlines on both sides of Lake Ontario.

"We just set the biggest bear trap of all time," the confident Gibson was quoted after the game.

In spite of the dramatic victory, the Tigers still trailed Toronto by 2 1/2 games with only seven to play.

"I just threw it out there," Gibson explained. "I probably should have said, 'Hey, you know, we don't have a chance.' But that was '87, so let's say we do. That's the way that team was. Even if we had no business saying it, we did say it and forced ourselves to do it. Amazing what people can do when they believe in themselves."

After splitting a four-game series with Baltimore, the

Tigers prepared to entertain the Blue Jays in the final three games of the season. The Blue Jays had gone to Milwaukee, where they dropped three straight games. They came to Detroit, leading by one game.

As with the four games the previous weekend, again all three were decided by one run. The Tigers won the opener, 4–3. They took 12 innings to snatch the second game, 3–2. In the season finale on a sunny Sunday afternoon, Frank Tanana used a Larry Herndon home run to finesse his way to a 1–0 victory. The impossible dream was complete. The Tigers were headed to Minnesota for the Playoffs.

Certainly the Tigers wanted to run the season longer. They were eliminated by the Twins, however, in five games.

"We were disappointed," Sparky said. "But it really didn't matter. Those seven games with Toronto were the best seven of my career. When I look back on that year, I still feel a high. The guys on that team can be proud of themselves for the rest of their lives."

Only two years later, Sparky paid a price for that precious piece of euphoria. Even today, some of those memories still live, too.

In 1989, the Tigers lost 103 games. While Tiger fans try never to remember the fiasco, the year remains unforgettable for Sparky. It's a Freddy Kreuger nightmare that never fully disappears.

Early in the season he finally came face-to-face with a relentless demon that had consumed his entire life.

This time the demon won.

Throughout his life, Sparky was obsessed with winning. This time that obsession demanded its pound of flesh.

Not just for the season in which the Tigers struggled, but for all those years in which Sparky had driven himself right up to the edge.

As with most personal conflicts, there was no single incident that cracked his limit of tolerance. A combination of factors festered, then leveled the seemingly invincible Sparky.

A plague of early season injuries to a variety of key players grounded the Tigers at 11 games under .500 by May

17th. Sparky kept spinning like a car sliding on ice, still trying to fulfill every charity and media request.

All the while, a family situation 2,000 miles away at home in California nibbled at Sparky's soul. Sparky's only daughter, Shirlee, was enduring a personal crisis of her own. She was pregnant at the time her first husband walked away from the family. Her vulnerability was shared by her father, who already felt helpless from grappling with a team that was falling apart.

Sparky's long-time feelings of guilt for being away so much from his family finally became too heavy to carry. Coupled with a crumbling team, the crack was unavoidable.

Sparky already had established himself as one of baseball's best managers in history. None was better at riding a good team to the limit. He had no peers at making an average team finish a little higher than anyone expected.

But not even Sparky could make a bad team look good.

In 1989, the truth of that reality came crashing down.

Except for a modest four-game winning streak toward the end of April, the team had struggled from the start. The needle in the eye occurred on May 11th at Toledo when the Tigers were humiliated in an exhibition game with their Class AAA affiliate.

On the bus ride to Cleveland where the Tigers headed for a three-game series, Sparky simply stared out the window at the desolate freeway. Unfamiliar forces squeezed at his insides. The longest week of his career had begun.

When he arrived in the Cleveland hotel, he had no chance at falling asleep. He merely sat in a chair and sweated. His shirt was wetter than one just out of the washer.

The Tigers lost two of three at Cleveland. They returned home and actually took two of three from Chicago. But the damage already had been done.

Sparky had agreed to appear at a charity function for Children's Hospital on Thursday's off-day. The function was fine.

Having to play Sparky again for a gaggle of fawning people, however, provided the knockout blow.

Sparky, as usual, was charming. Everyone left feeling good. He shook every hand. He flashed his disarming smile. He appeared to be vintage Sparky. Win or lose, the show went on.

When he returned home that evening, though, he knew something was drastically wrong. He wrestled with his demon while sitting in the living room. After forcing himself to walk upstairs for bed, he fell into an ugly sleep.

He was awakened the next morning by a phone call from Tiger President Jim Campbell. From Sparky's conversation, Campbell knew something was wrong.

"I didn't know what it was," Campbell explained. "But something wasn't right. That wasn't the real Sparky talking."

Campbell immediately called team physician Dr. Clarence Livingood. Within the next couple of hours, it had been determined that Sparky should return to his home in Thousand Oaks for rest.

The Tigers announced that their manager was suffering from exhaustion. The malady, of course, was as much mental as it was physical.

For Sparky the unthinkable happened. He had to leave his team in the middle of a season.

From the High Side and Low

The good ones have the guts to stick out the bad times. The great ones have the will to make the good times even better.

The trick is how we deal with adversity. How we handle success is the yardstick of character.

Wouldn't it get boring if there were no hills to climb? Without no tears, we might never know how good it feels to smile. A loss don't mean surrender. It's only a reminder to appreciate our gifts.

After winning three World Series, I think I got spoiled. If you don't dance with the queen of the prom, what's the sense of even going out on the floor? That's the way I used to think.

Then along came 1987 and I learned one of the greatest lessons of my life.

Winning the division had nothing to do with it. We could have lost it on that last weekend and I wouldn't have been less proud of that team.

That team didn't realize it wasn't that good. They just refused to quit.

We didn't make it to the World Series, but they proved to me they were champions. A true champion is someone who gets up even when he can't. And that's what they did all year long.

I wish every youngster and every person who thinks about giving up could have watched that team. To be a winner, all you have to give is all you've got. When that season ended, their bodies were empty.

For pure physical talent, that team was grayer than a three-piece suit.

The difference was their heart. No one realized just how big it was.

Down deep, those guys knew they weren't as good as the final record showed. But standings never show what's inside a guy's heart. That's something I wish every person would learn regardless what they do in life. Work as hard as you can and never look back. Then let somebody else worry about what happens.

I used to have a sign hanging in my office. It said: "A miracle can happen. Always believe in miracles."

That team made a believer out of me. I got the Manager of the Year Award. It should be engraved with the names of every one of those guys. Then they should hang the thing in Cooperstown to show kids what can happen if you ain't afraid of failing.

At the beginning of each year I told my teams it didn't matter where they finished. If they played as hard as they could, they could look at themselves and be proud of what they saw in the mirror.

Those guys can walk proud for the rest of their lives. At least for that one year, no team showed more heart.

There was nobody more surprised than me when 1987 finally ended. Every spring I used to tell Carol and Dan Ewald exactly where I thought we'd finish. I never told the writers, but I picked that team to finish fourth.

All of a sudden funny things started to happen. Once in a while every team catches a streak where everything goes right. That year, though, the bag of goodies never got empty.

Roger Craig (former Tiger pitching coach who was managing San Francisco) called near the end of the season. He wanted to know how we were doing it.

"Roger, you ain't got enough time in your life and I

ain't got enough in mine to explain what's going on," I told him. "I'm seeing it, but I don't believe it."

There were actually times when I felt like asking those guys, "Do you know you're not supposed to be in this position?" They just found a way to pull out every close game. Sometimes, I swear, Harry Houdini was somewhere out on the field.

It was the best bunting team I ever had. It was the best hit-and-run team I ever had. They did something else better than any team I ever had. They tolerated each other like no other team I ever saw.

Off the field, they weren't best buddies. Some guys would go one way and some would go another. Once they got in that clubhouse, though, you could feel the change. Once they started to prepare to walk past those white lines, they were all business. Everybody was one. If they were gonna win, they were gonna win together. If they were gonna lose, they were gonna lose together, too.

Nothing ever bothered them. It never mattered what the writers wrote or whether anybody else believed. They believed in themselves. That's all that mattered.

When we lost those first three games in Toronto at the end of the season, it really didn't bother me. How could it? Those guys had given so much all year. They had done far more than anything I asked.

If that club had wound up losing to the Blue Jays, I would have felt just as proud of them today. I know when that season ended, there wasn't an ounce of energy left in any of them.

In my 43 years in baseball I never saw nothing like those seven games with Toronto. Every game was settled by one run. The games were played out of a textbook.

When Gibson talked about setting that trap, I thought he was crazy. I'll never be able to thank that team enough for the way they never quit. It still gives me a high today.

I get just the opposite feeling when I think about what happened two years later.

Baseball was made to break your heart. If you think you're destined never to fail, you better keep one eye open when you fall asleep at night.

That ain't feeling sorry for yourself. That's just the way life is.

For my first 19 years as a manager I was blessed by so much good fortune I thought maybe the devil had forgotten where I lived. In 1989, I found out that Sparky Anderson has to pay his dues, too.

It don't matter how big you think you are. You ain't never bigger than all the people around you. So just be grateful for the good things you got.

It was scary. I'll never forget the day I left. Riding down those streets on my way to the airport, I kept thinking to myself I'd never see them again. All the good times . . . all the tough times . . . they were all gone. I thought I'd never manage again.

I kept asking myself—how can a major league manager leave his team on May 19th to go home?

I found out why. Because it's humanly impossible to push a person past all the limits of physical and mental reality and not pay the devil his price.

Even a character like Sparky. He has his limits, too.

I finally faced facts. And it was the best thing that ever happened to me.

I thought I could do everything. Every interview. Every appearance. Every charity function. I thought I could do all that and make a major league team finish a little higher than it was supposed to.

There's a difference between pushing yourself to the limit and fooling yourself into thinking that the limits don't apply to you. That 1987 Tiger team took winning to the limit. I thought I could take it a step further where everybody else was afraid to walk.

That's what I did with winning. Winning had consumed me ever since I was a boy.

Until that year, I didn't want to talk to nobody after a loss. I talked to the press because it was my job. When that was over, I felt it was time for a little piece of me to die.

Whenever we lost, I felt like I had let so many people down. I felt like everything depended on Sparky and he had to be in complete control.

Until 1989, I blamed myself for every loss. It was time for me to set my priorities straight. Why did I let something like 1989 have to show me how foolish I had been?

I finally came to realize that all the good years weren't just because of me. Neither were the tough times I was facing. I just had to work them through.

Until then, I never dreamed I could ever be part of a team that couldn't play at least .500 ball. I was embarrassed and ashamed.

I should have been embarrassed for the way I reacted. No person—not even Sparky—can do any more than what the Good Lord has blessed him with.

We don't succeed in life only because of ourselves. We succeed from the combined efforts of everybody around us. You can't have a fancy car without a good tail light. Every little part makes the whole picture right.

I learned to appreciate the problems other people face. For the first time I really understood that old saying about the man who quit complaining about a pair of new shoes when he walked past a person who only had one leg.

Feeling sorry for yourself is a lonely proposition. Lend a hand to someone in trouble and you'll never be alone.

A problem at work ain't no more than a one-day headache. You think parents with a terminally ill child worry about a problem at the office?

From that time forward, I tried to put every losing streak in its place. I knew the next day we always had a chance of winning. When a blind man goes to sleep at night, he knows he ain't got no chance of seeing when the morning comes around.

Those are the bravest people in the world. Life ain't easy for them, but they know what's important.

When I got home and saw that my daughter was all right, I knew all the other stuff didn't mean a thing.

Sure the games mattered. I never entered one that I didn't do everything I could to win. When your family is healthy, though, I don't care if you're the manager of a baseball team or a riveter on the assembly line, your problems ain't nothing. They're only in the way.

I knew I had to work on letting go of that obsession to win. I also knew I had to prove to myself I could do it.

I taught myself to accept the fact there would be a tomorrow. More than that, I wanted tomorrow to come. God never promised us happiness. All He promised was the opportunity to achieve it. The rest is up to us. That's the promise of tomorrow.

I spent 17 days away from my team. I went back to Detroit on June 5th when Boston was in town. I wanted to return to the team in Detroit. That's where I left them and that's where I had to go back.

The fans were super. There were "Welcome Back Sparky" signs around the park. I tried to acknowledge all of them.

We got beat that night. In fact, we didn't win too many more all year. We finished with a 59–103 record and deserved every loss.

I knew for sure nobody could have been treated better in any other city when the Governor of the state had a "Sparky Anderson Day" in September.

I had to be the luckiest guy in baseball. What other manager could take a two-week "vacation" in the middle of the season and then get honored by the governor?

I never got over the point of bleeding a little inside after every loss. If a manager or player ever loses that edge, then it's time to get out of the game.

But I finally learned to let go. I gave up that obsession for always having control.

I learned to practice what I had preached all the time. I still don't know why it takes a disaster to make some people realize how much they've really been blessed.

I can't say I'm happy with the pain I went through in 1989. But I'm grateful for what it taught me. I hope young people learn from my lesson and not have to fight through an ugly one of their own.

My greatest gift today is knowing I have a tomorrow. And I always want it to come.

From the Kids

Sparky used the same approach to baseball he uses for playing a round of golf . . . or caring for his cherished collection of plants in the backyard . . . or even just brushing his teeth.

He never tiptoes around to the back. He squares his shoulders and comes charging through the front door.

"If you gotta get to someplace, there ain't no sense walking sideways," Sparky says.

There's no low, medium, and high speeds in Sparky's life. He runs on "boil" whether he's washing his car in the driveway or contemplating an eighth inning pitching change in the seventh game of the World Series.

Even simple tasks are tackled head-on. There may not be a next time.

Calculated recklessness is part of life, according to Sparky. It's essential to the character. It's part of the Sparky mystique.

Sparky is grateful for his telephone-book-size of baseball accomplishments. He now can appreciate the mistakes he learned to turn into triumphs. He never wastes a second worrying about "should have dones" and "could have beens."

"What's the sense about crying about a hole in the bucket?" he asks. "All that's gonna do is keep you from fixing it."

After winning back-to-back World Championships, the personal legend of Sparky began to assume a life of its own.

The price of legend, however, never is cheap. Although he judges himself far harsher than any of his children, Sparky still can't shake the single regret which has haunted him throughout his career.

"I cheated my kids out of a lot of quality time when they were young," Sparky admits. "I don't sit around and think about it all the time. But it's there. I can't get that time back, so I don't beat myself down every day. But I'm sorry for it."

Those who followed a similar path to celebrity empathize with Sparky's feelings. Just as quickly, though, they hail Sparky's compassion for people more than any self-perceived shortcoming.

"There's no question Sparky chose a profession that required a lot of travel and time away from home," said Bo Schembechler. "But you have to look at the whole man. Look at how much good feeling he has generated for people all over the country.

"There is nothing on this earth that Sparky regards higher than his family. He's always provided for them. He still does. He was always there whenever they needed him."

Bo's rigid test of character puts Sparky at the head of the class.

"Nobody in sports has lived a more exemplary life than Sparky Anderson," Bo said. "He's a family man and a churchgoing man. There's never been the hint of scandal around him. And nobody is as generous with charity work as Sparky. I think he's given himself to so many people rather than taken himself from his family."

Growing up as the child of any celebrated performer presents as many peculiar pressures as it does privileges. Growing up as the son or daughter of a bona fide baseball legend known as Sparky is even more peculiar.

Sparky and Carol have two grown sons and one grown daughter. Lee is the oldest, followed by Shirlee and Albert. All are married with children of their own.

"You can't regret those days," Shirlee said. 'Kids grow up and learn how to live through those things. Being the girl, I never resented the fact that my father was gone. I always was sad the day he went to spring training. But 24 hours later, I was happy for him.

"I'm awfully happy he did what he did. He never did it

selfishly. My father never worked for the wrong reasons. He wasn't going away to forget about his family. He was doing it to provide for his family the best way he knew how. He wasn't that educated and he was doing something he loved so much. That's a pretty neat thing. Especially the way he brought so much happiness to so many people and never changed as a person."

Shirlee has three children—Shelley, Daniel, and Steven—from her first marriage. She and her husband, Jan, have Emily and Jansen between them. Jan has four children—Jexson, Tovah, Jordan, and Tabitha—from his first marriage.

"I was always so happy to see my father doing what he loved," Shirlee said. "A lot of my friends' parents hated to go to work. My father never came home from work and opened up a bottle to cover up the woes. I'm so pleased I never had that.

"I always knew if there was a crisis—if I really needed him—he would be there. He did it more than once. He made me feel good just to know he was doing something that made him happy. And he was so good at it."

Lee and his wife, Dawn, have four children in their home. Georgie is Lee's son from a previous marriage. Dawn has Amy, Danielle, and Elizabeth from a previous marriage. Lee admits that, as a boy, he missed his father when he was gone. But he also understands.

"Dad being gone probably bothered me more when I was a teen-ager and he was managing in the big leagues," Lee said. "It was different because my dad was so strict when he came home. I did pretty much what I wanted to do when he was gone. I was the oldest and the defiant one.

"Now that I'm 39 and have my own family, I can put all the pieces together. Dad was only doing what he had to do. I know how tough it must have been on him. I've got a five-year-old that really cares for me. I wouldn't want to be away from her that much."

Albert and wife, Sarah, have one son—Todd. Albert also admits to having missed his father at times. It wasn't until he became an adult, though, that he truly grasped baseball's unusual lifestyle.

"Now that I have a child myself, I wouldn't be able to be away from him so long," Albert said. "When I was a kid, though, I never wondered why dad was gone. I knew why he was gone. It made perfect sense to me. He wasn't gone for any bad reason. Baseball was a good thing to be away for."

Lee and Albert agree that their father's time in the minor leagues was more enjoyable for them than when he made it to the majors. There was more time "to hang around with dad." There were more opportunities for personal interaction. The major leagues are much more restrictive.

"I remember when I was five years old and Dad managed the St. Petersburg, Florida team," Lee said. "I was the batboy. We won the second half championship and I got beer poured all over my head in the clubhouse.

"I also remember shagging flies before the games. We used to go out to the park real early. My dad and I would walk around the infield picking up rocks. He was probably the best grounds crew hand any stadium had.

"I thought it was neat for a kid to hang around the park with those young players. But my father always pushed my brother and me away from a baseball career. He saw no future in it as far as family life. He wanted us to have nine-to-five jobs so we could be home all year round with our kids and families."

Albert also treasures his memories of his father's minor league days.

"I enjoyed all his years at Cincinnati and Detroit because they meant so much to him," Albert said. "But they weren't as exciting as when he was in the minor leagues. I remember hitting balls into the screen before the games when he managed at Asheville. That's when I really enjoyed going to the park."

Away from the park, the Anderson children were always cautious never to use their father's influence to benefit their own affairs.

"It was tough in a way, but easier in a lot of other ways," Lee said. "Even to this day, I still run into people who want to meet him. But none of us ever played the 'Dad card.' My parents weren't that way. None of us were."

For the most part, Sparky and Carol kept their children in California schools. For the last few months of the school year one time, the three children switched to schools in Cincinnati.

"We agreed we wouldn't say who our dad was," Albert said. "Not because we weren't proud, but we didn't want the attention.

"The first day at school, the kids asked what my dad did. I said he was a manager. They said manager of what? I said a baseball manager. Finally they figured out he managed the Reds. From that day on it was difficult to be at school because people would always point at you and ask why the team lost yesterday."

Albert confirmed the fact that kids often sought his association merely because of his father's position.

"There were some kids like that," he said. "But it never worked on me. Most of my friends were my friends before he ever got to the big leagues."

Simply participating in sports also carried an additional burden for Lee and Albert.

"I always got moved along too fast in my Little League career," Lee recalled. "I got pushed up in leagues because of who my father was. The other managers always wanted to put me above the levels where I should have been. It was tough. Some of the coaches would take things out on me. I wound up quitting baseball and didn't play again till I joined an over-30 league."

Regardless of the peculiar pressures that affect the children of a legitimate sports legend, neither Lee nor Shirlee nor Albert would trade either of their parents for anyone in the world.

"I was blessed with two great guardian angels," Lee said. "I love them both with my whole heart. Dad comes from the old school. It doesn't matter what rung of the ladder you come from. He's nice to everybody. He's going to treat you the same way he treats everybody else. To know him is a blessing."

All three kids also learned as much from the legend's "other half."

"My mom is special," Lee explained. "She's the direct opposite of Dad. She thinks everything out before making a decision. She's patient and very wise.

"When Dad was gone, she took on the role of both parents. She devoted her whole life to the family. No problem was ever too small or too big for her to handle. She did it so quietly. She never breathed to a soul who our father is."

Carol, in fact, is as proud of her husband's accomplishments as he is. But she is equally proud of her own identity and that of her family's.

"Don't ever make the mistake of calling her 'Mrs. Sparky Anderson,'" Sparky explains. "She's Carol Anderson. She's earned that."

Albert admits to carrying numerous lessons that he's learned from his famous father and his unheralded mother. She's the perfect foil to Sparky.

"The main thing I carry, for sure, is how nice my mom and dad are to people," Albert said. "I would never think of hurting another person. I learned that from them. They're the two nicest people I know. That's the best quality anybody can have. I hope I give that to my son. Treat people like you want to be treated. Like my dad says, that will never cost a dime."

Shirlee is blessed with the bubbly personality of her father and the quiet wisdom of her much more reserved mom.

"My dad taught me to love who I am and live my own life properly," Shirlee said. "My mom has given me so much insight into so many aspects of life.

"My mom has so much patience. She will sit down and plan things out. She'll think about how it should be done correctly. She'll take four straight steps whereas Dad just does things. He'll go down the block and across the street and over the hill to finally get to where he's going. He likes the motion. They're exactly the same, though, when it comes to support and giving love."

Shirlee is appreciatively sensitive to the way Sparky has

grown into becoming a real grandfather to all 14 of his grandkids.

"I have one daughter who can charm anything out of him . . . and he just loves it," Shirlee said. "He's doing more with them now than he ever did.

"I love my grandparents. But I don't think they taught my dad that it's O.K. to hug and it's O.K. to sit down on the floor and act silly. Now he acts a little too silly with some of mine. He's doing things he would have never done before. Not because he was a bad father, but because he didn't know how to do those things before. He had to support his family. Things have changed so much . . . and all for the better."

Maybe it's because Sparky has more time to spend with his children and their children. Maybe it's because he's making more time.

Whatever the reason, Sparky thoroughly enjoys his "play time" with the grandkids.

Lee and his family live only a 20-minute ride from Carol and Sparky's house and frequently visit. Shirlee and Albert both live in the area near Sacramento. Several times during the year, Carol and Sparky drive the several hour trip so Sparky can play grandfather.

Perhaps one of the best gifts Sparky gave his kids came after the 1996 season when he didn't get the Anaheim Angels managing job for which it appeared he was in the running.

"When he told me about the Angels, I told him I hoped he wouldn't take it," Lee said. "I didn't want him to go back to baseball. I know he enjoyed it and that was what his life was about, but I was glad to see him wear shorts and play golf and play with his grandkids.

"He doesn't need baseball anymore. He does TV for Angels' home games. That's enough and he's still around the game. I'm glad he doesn't have to do it the whole season."

Albert never expressed his feelings personally to his father, but they echo Lee's. In fact, he feels a sense of relief.

"Whatever was best for him, I wanted him to do," Albert said. "But he's earned his time to enjoy himself.

"It's easier for me not to read the sports section everyday. When one of his teams went on a seven-game losing streak it felt more personal to me even though it shouldn't have. I took the losses too hard. When he's not managing, I don't even have to read the sports pages."

Certainly Sparky has regrets over lost time with his children. Those feelings are personal. Nothing will change them.

But he's never failed to place love for his family above everything else in life. As a national celebrity, he's also spread that warmth to an extended family all across the nation.

And as Shirlee figures, "That's a pretty neat thing to do."

Better Late than Never

The best thing about Carol Anderson is that she ain't a lick impressed by Sparky.

She loves the real me. As long as I made an honest living, she never cared less if I was written up in the newspapers or if I was delivering them.

She ain't into the glamour thing. I already had won a couple of world championships and she still worked as a cashier at the drug store down the street. She just felt like she wanted to do something. And nobody at the store knew her husband was this Sparky guy.

I'll never forget the time she told me—you're not God in this house. She never plays games. She's always straight up.

In the business I was in, a lot of guys played mind games with you. They tried to make you think they were coming east when actually they were circling the wagons and coming west.

Not Carol. She gives it to you straight.

She appreciates what baseball has meant to our family. But she appreciates more what the family means to all of us. She's the one who deserves the credit for our three children turning out so good.

Carol and I met back in the fifth grade. We hung around together way back then. We got married on October 3rd, 1953. We built the house we live in back in 1967 and we ain't never gonna move.

She's done so much for me. One of those modern exploding scoreboards couldn't total up everything. The best thing she ever did was the way she raised my two boys and daughter. Without her, things would have been a real mess.

Carol is the one with all the common sense in our house. I don't know how she made it through 43 years in professional baseball. She raised Lee, Shirlee, and Albert.

When there were parent-teacher meetings at school, Carol was there. When Shirlee was having "boy" troubles, Carol was there. When one of the kids had to be rushed to the doctor, Carol was there. When one of the kids just needed someone they could trust and talk to, Carol was there.

And then there was me. I was her biggest project.

When clubs weren't going right, sometimes I acted like a madman. I'd worry about this and get mad about that. Carol never wavered. No one else could have put up with me and have the strength to raise three kids as well as she did.

Those three kids mean the world to me. Lee is marvelous. He's one of the hardest workers you'll ever see. If he has any faults, it's that he's too generous. He's got a concrete finishing business and he's always giving everything away. That's just the way he is.

Shirlee is twice the ball of energy I am. She's a machine that don't have no stop switch.

I don't know how she does it. She's thirty-seven years old . . . has nine kids . . . and she don't look a minute over twenty-two. Obviously she didn't get that last trait from me.

The most beautiful part about her is that she is so comfortable with who she is. She loves herself. And that love radiates to everybody she touches.

Albert reminds me so much of Carol. He's much quieter than me and the other kids. He doesn't love anything more than being home with his wife, Sarah, and their boy, Todd. Albert needs nothing. Material things mean nothing to him. He's a very precious person.

I am very blessed that my children turned out to be so good. That ain't because of me. It's because Carol dug in when the going got tough.

I've gotten extremely close to my kids now. But I missed all the years from the time they were four years old till they were twenty-four. I provided for them. We had some good times. But I never gave them me. I'm sorry for that. I've got no one to blame but myself.

What if I am fortunate enough to go into the Hall of Fame? I hope that I am.

But when I look back on all the World Series and all the All-Star Games and all the television and newspaper publicity and all the people I've met . . . it wasn't worth all of what I took from the kids.

I can't reach into a magic hat and get those times back. Nobody can. Not even Sparky. So there's no sense crying about it.

It's better to be honest with yourself and admit a mistake instead of wasting even more time worrying about something you can't control.

That's why I want for all young people who read this to learn a lesson I had to pay for.

Don't shed no tears when your kids are gone and you're sixty years old. You might not believe it now, but I guarantee you that day will come. Don't miss the airplane trying to catch a star.

Enjoy yourself with those kids when you're 25 or 30 or 35 or 40. Take care of all your business, but make those kids so close that they're almost part of you.

That's the time they need you the most. If you help them grow and gain the confidence they need as youngsters, you won't have no worries when it's time for them to make it on their own.

Don't get me wrong. I don't stay awake at night and torment myself about it. What's the sense in kicking myself? I know the truth. I don't tell myself a lie. If you're gonna tell lies, you're gonna mess up the chance of making it any better.

Tell yourself the truth. And the truth is simple. Every doctor, lawyer, and Indian chief—I don't care what you do for a living—can do the job at work and do the job with the kids. That's just a total lie if somebody says they didn't have the time.

Get out of bed an hour earlier. Work an hour later after the kids go to sleep.

If you have kids, you must somehow make the time. Those kids belong to you and everybody's future.

There are no jobs that should take away all of your time from the kids. That's where people are wrong. That's the greatest alibi in the world. Alibis are for losers and people who don't care about the truth.

I could have made more time. It wouldda taken a little more work on my part, but I couldda done it. The alibi is easy once the time is over. Do it right the first time and then you don't never have to look back.

If you want to chase a dream and do something a little bit different than other people, that's all right. You have to work like a dog and sometimes you have to bleed.

But save some of that blood for your family. The job will always be there. Those kids are gonna grow up some day.

It's O.K. for young parents to work for that big house in the suburbs. It's O.K. to buy a fancy second car. It's O.K. to work extra hard for one more promotion. Just remember, no amount of money can ever buy back the time they miss with their kids.

Ball players and doctors and lawyers and salesmen and all kinds of jobs can steal away a lot of time. They trick you into thinking you are a little more important than you really are.

I once heard a story about a fascinating older lady

who was asked if she might be interested in writing her autobiography. She smiled. Very calmly she replied, "People tend to think their lives are a little more important than they really are."

That lady never wasted any of her life.

The trick is not to let your pocket get picked before you know what happened. There's nothing wrong with sacrificing for your career. But don't make the kids part of that sacrifice. That ain't working hard . . . that's simply being selfish.

I never did nothing bad to embarrass my family or baseball. But I did take the easy route and kept driving toward my goal. I cheated my kids out of too much precious time. Now no amount of awards can ever get it back.

It's doubly tough for kids growing up with a father or mother who is famous. I don't think I ever realized just how tough it was on my kids. People expect the kids to be something they're not.

When my two boys were playing ball, they never wanted me to come to their games. When I showed up, all the other kids wanted my autograph. Their coaches always expected my boys to be so much better than the talent they had.

That's why Carol was so important to all of us. She never allowed any of the outside influences to affect the kids.

Carol never let them take special privileges just because I was Sparky. Whatever they got, Carol made sure they earned it on their own.

My children were the same way. They never let on that their father was Sparky. They made friends on their own terms.

Our house was always filled with kids from the neighborhood. But if anybody made a fuss because I was around, it was the last time those kids were ever invited. I'm proud of my kids for that.

I thank God that all three of my children have grown to be good responsible parents themselves.

I know I've looked like an old-timer my whole life. I just never thought of myself as becoming a real grandfather. Now I can't believe how much fun it really is. I've been able to do a few things for them that somewhere down the road, my grandkids will know that grandma and grandpa were around. I only wish I would have known enough about it to do some of those things right from the start.

I urge young parents never to let the time slip by before it's too late. Do things right the first time around. There ain't no second shots in this game, so you better make the first one.

Money can't fix the problems. That's the biggest mistake any young parents can make. Having a good loving family means you don't have nothing to fix.

When they lay you in that box, there ain't gonna be no money or cars or houses around. Any awards you might have picked up along the way ain't going in that box with you. And all the green flies that used to hang around are gonna be busy looking for someone else to latch on to.

The family will be there. I thank God for the beautiful one I have. Without them, I know Sparky would have been as empty as Yankee Stadium on New Year's Day.

Sparky's Greatest Gift

Sparky pulled a rabbit out of his hat by leading the 1987 Tigers to a division championship. The summer of magic carved warm memories that are still alive today.

What he managed to create off the field that year, though, will live even longer. Thousands of underprivileged Detroit kids and their families defy anyone to call it anything but a miracle.

During the heat of one of the most unpredictable pennant drives in Tiger history, Sparky somehow pieced together a dream.

It's a dream that makes a baseball championship seem no more than a Friday night at the movies.

"His managerial records are unchallenged," said longtime Tiger team physician Dr. Clarence Livingood. "He is, without doubt, Hall of Fame timber. But this man will be remembered more for what he did with CATCH than for anything he did on the field. I don't know how he did it, but he truly created a miracle."

CATCH is an acronym for Caring Athletes Team for Children's and Henry Ford Hospitals. Its mission is dedicated to improving the quality of life of pediatric patients at the two Detroit inner-city hospitals. The aim is to provide needy pediatric patients with assistance not otherwise available.

The beautiful part about the charity is, as Sparky says, "It works without all the red tape."

Sparky admits that piecing everything together in the frenzy of a surprise pennant drive probably was "a little bit crazy." But all the pieces fit. Against some pretty steep odds, CATCH became, as Dr. Livingood describes, "a living blessing."

"Sparky always was sincere about helping players," said Kirk Gibson. "I think as he got older, he realized he had so much more to give to so many more people.

"His whole life had been the game. Then something hit him. Baseball isn't the only thing in the world. He felt he was in the position to reach out and touch people beyond the game. I don't think he realized the momentum it would pick up because he's such a humble guy. Everybody knew it was going to be huge except for Sparky. He simply said, 'I'll do what I can.'"

Sparky and his army of volunteers far surpassed their original expectations. In fact, no one imagined how far-reaching the charity would become.

CATCH already has issued grants of more than $1.5 million. It has an endowment of about $3 million to ensure the organization's perpetuity. Through a variety of annual fund-raising events, the endowment continues to grow.

The numbers are as impressive as Sparky's baseball records. The fact that Sparky was able to pull off the miracle is a miracle itself.

"He became driven to get CATCH set up," recalls Jack Morris. "I think it actually helped him during that pennant race. Somehow he was able to stay focused on both things."

Sparky always had a marshmallow heart for anything pertaining to kids. Throughout his managerial career, he always made time to visit them in the local hospitals. He did it during the glory years at Cincinnati. He continued through the hectic championship years and the disappointing down days at Detroit.

In Detroit, Sparky's hospital visits turned into pizza parties for the kids. When Tom Monaghan owned the Tigers, Sparky arranged for free pizza to be delivered. Monaghan, of course, is the owner of Domino's Pizza.

Visits were made discreetly. In fact, he threatened hospital officials that the visits would cease if he showed up to a group of reporters and cameramen.

Instead of dollars, sometimes players' fines came in the

form of mandatory hospital visits. Sparky then would be escorted into children's wards with some of the game's brightest stars.

More often than not, players left the hospital a little teary-eyed. And almost always, those visits planted the seeds for future voluntary returns.

For whatever reason, Sparky felt he had not reached out far enough to the community. He wasn't sure exactly what it might be, but he was certain there was more that he could do.

The trigger for action occurred shortly after the 1987 season began.

Before home night games, Sparky often visited a neighborhood men's clothing store where he shared coffee with owner Hank Simonovich and his sons, Steve and Frank.

On one particular morning when Sparky went into the back room where Hank altered suits on his sewing machine, the store owner hugged Sparky and broke down crying. He told Sparky that his grandson, David, was hospitalized. He had been diagnosed as having leukemia.

Sparky immediately called David and promised to visit him after the team returned from its road trip. He also made a promise to himself. Somehow he was going to do something to help kids who were not fortunate enough to help themselves.

The first stop on the trip was Seattle. At 6 a.m. on April 27th, Sparky took the first step toward making his promise come to life.

He jumped out of bed and began to scribble plans for a sports memorabilia auction. All proceeds would benefit hospitalized underprivileged children. By 8 a.m., he had run out of paper. He asked a maid for another pad. He didn't finish writing notes until almost 9 o'clock.

"I had so many things spinning in my head, the C.I.A. couldn't have figured them all out," Sparky recalls.

After returning from the road trip, Sparky shared his idea with Dr. Livingood. The two met with officials from Henry Ford and Children's Hospitals.

"To be truthful, the hospitals were very cool on the idea,"

Sparky explained. "They thought they were dealing with a nut. They were skeptical about this memorabilia thing raising any kind of significant money. Well, when it was all done, we suddenly became the fair-haired people. Then the thing just snowballed."

Sparky put together a team of volunteers like Dr. Livingood, Bob and Phyllis Pilcowitz, Jerry and Shirley Shagrin and several others. He also rolled up his sleeves and collected a garage full of signed memorabilia items for public auction. Items were collected from every celebrated star in every professional sport. The collection even included a baseball jersey with the signatures of President Ronald Reagan and his wife, Nancy.

With almost the entire Tiger team attending the affair to sign free autographs, the auction generated more than $190,000 to be distributed equally to the two hospitals.

Blind determination definitely paid off. CATCH quickly became one of the community's more prominent charities. It attracted the interest of Alan Frank, who agreed to serve as CATCH chairman. Frank is general manager of WDIV-TV, Detroit's NBC affiliate, which provided a valuable publicity vehicle. Now serving as Chairman is Edsel Ford, president of the Ford Motor Credit Corporation and an heir to the Ford Motor Company fortune.

CATCH has been able to attract and maintain the support of several locally prominent business executives who have lifted the charity to a level Sparky never dreamed possible.

But the real story lies in the children and the families that CATCH continues to serve. Examples of how CATCH funds are used include:

- A teen-age boy with multiple disabilities, including cerebral palsy and impaired lower extremities, benefited from a chair lift which eased his transportation to and from his second-story bedroom. The need for the lift was intensified when the boy's father was murdered in a senseless act of violence.

- While a child suffered through a fatal illness, his father wished to spend as much time as possible with his son. To do so, he was forced to take an unpaid leave of absence from work. CATCH funds were used to pay for one month's rent so that he did not miss the last days of his child's life.
- A boy diagnosed with cancer fell far behind his school work because of lengthy hospitalizations. His dream had been to graduate with the classmates he grew up with. In order to do so, he had to enroll in a summer school program that his family could not afford. CATCH paid for the program and he was able to graduate on time, making the last 18 months of his life complete.
- CATCH funds were used to replace Christmas toys for a youngster with a brain tumor who was hospitalized when his home was burglarized during the holidays.

"CATCH is a charity that really does help sick children in need," said Henry Ford Hospital social worker Mary Otto. "There are so many examples.

"Last year there was a toddler who died in our Intensive Care Unit. The mother called me periodically afterward. She was trying to adjust to the loss of her little girl. She was having the hardest time over the fact that there was no marker on the grave. When she and the other children visited the cemetery, this tore at her heart. She didn't have the 'pay in advance' money the cemetery required, and the state doesn't help.

"CATCH funds paid for a small grave marker, and the last time the mom called me she expressed her heartfelt thanks for the marker. She at last had felt closure and peace."

The stories are countless. Although Sparky no longer maintains a residence in Detroit, he still remains active in a variety of CATCH activities.

"Even though Sparky is gone from the day-to-day operation, CATCH continues to flourish," said Executive Director

Jim Hughes. "That speaks volumes, not only of Sparky, but how his sincerity toward the well-being of children is received in our community. Some people lend their name to a charity or a cause. With CATCH, Sparky brings work and wisdom. He's extremely generous with each."

As he attributes his professional success to his players on the field, Sparky points to all the volunteers for the success of the charity that remains so close to his heart.

Without his determination to touch some youngsters who otherwise couldn't help themselves, his dream would never have become a reality.

All the baseball record books loudly assure Sparky's niche of immortality. All those individuals touched by this charity silently affirm something more important than any baseball honor.

Without a doubt, Sparky wouldn't trade CATCH for anything in the world.

For the Children

If you reach out to help a child, I promise you that when you put your head down on that pillow at night, you're gonna sleep with the angels.

A man never stands so tall as when he stoops down to help a child.

No feeling in the world can come close. That single precious moment can mean a lifetime for a child.

We all must remember that a child has no face. A child only has an outline. People paint in the face. That child don't know and could care less what his or her face looks like.

A child is not a child because it's black. A child is not a child because it's oriental. A child is not a child because it's white.

A child is a child because that's exactly what it is—a precious beautiful child. Us older folks paint in all the prejudices and all that other stuff. We're the ones who create all the trouble.

You could fill a big room with 200 children. All of them could speak a totally different language. None of them might understand what the next kid was saying. Leave them alone for a couple of hours and I guarantee that when you come back, they'll all be playing with each other. And there won't be no problems just because one is white and the other is black or somebody is speaking English and another is talking Spanish.

That's because they're children. They ain't been

around long enough to get polluted by all the stuff us grown-ups feed them.

Now what happens when some of these children get sick or their families run into problems where they can't afford to help them? Or what about some of these children who really don't have no families of their own?

Are we supposed to turn our heads and just say "too bad . . . that ain't none of my concern?"

Every one of those children is our child. They belong to all of us. Just because they don't have our names or we ain't their real mamas or daddies, they're still our children.

Every time I go to the hospital to visit those kids, I always realize that could be one of my very own. When a blind child walks up to me, I know that could have been Lee or Shirlee or Albert. When a youngster is so sick that he can't get out of bed and all he can do is to try to squeeze my hand, I thank God that hasn't happened to one of my kids or one of my grandkids. But it's still my child in a bigger sense. I still have an obligation to try to do whatever I can. We all do.

Whenever I go into any of those children's hospitals, I always walk away knowing those kids did more for me than I ever could do for them. They confirm my belief that every child belongs to all of us. They make me realize how fortunate all of us are.

That's why the creation of CATCH is the greatest accomplishment of my lifetime. It has nothing to do with me. It has nothing to do with my career. It has everything to do with the kids.

I don't know how it all happened. I don't know how I ever got so many big people to do all that they've done.

I never want to be able to put my finger on it. I always want to think of it as a miracle. It was a miracle and it happened. I'm gonna take credit for that miracle because that's one thing nobody can ever take away or second guess me on.

People can say I made a lot of mistakes managing. But nobody can ever say I made a mistake when I came up with CATCH.

It reminds me of how so many times in my career as a manager we'd run into some injuries. I'd have to slip in a player because I didn't have nobody else. Sometimes the player wound up being a star and made me look like a genius. Sometimes things that work out so good are the result of blind luck.

Well, I ain't gonna try to figure this one out. I'm just happy that the kids are the winners.

One of the things that really helped me get the charity going was the way the hospitals acted when Dr. Livingood and I first met with them. They were nice. They listened. But when I left, I kinda felt like they were laughing behind my back. They didn't think we could pull this thing off. They thought I was a legitimate head case.

When somebody puts a dare in my face like that and so much good for so many kids is on the line, I'm gonna take that dare and shove it down somebody's throat.

I'll take the credit for getting CATCH going. But none of this could have been done without all the unselfish sacrifices of so many people.

Alan Frank jumped in like Michael Jordan on a dunk shot. He gave us so much free TV time and organized all the details to make sure the charity would run forever.

Now we've got Edsel Ford as our chairman. He needs an extra job like this like he needs a recall on all of his new car models.

Here's a guy who comes from one of the wealthiest families in the country. But he cares about kids. He knows how important it is to help some people who only need a little hand.

I've always said that if there truly is a saint walking on this earth, his name is Clarence Livingood. Dr. Livingood don't know nothing but how to help anybody who needs a hand. He couldn't say "no" if that was the last word left in the dictionary.

CATCH just happens to be the charity that's closest to my heart. But it don't matter what charity somebody chooses or what kind of help they give. As long as people realize that all these kids belong to all of us, then it don't matter how we choose to help.

If people would just take a moment to realize that sometimes the littlest thing you do for a child is the biggest thing that child will ever receive.

Sometimes all it takes is a smile or a little wink of the eye. A little thing like that tells a kid you notice. What's wrong with letting a child know we care?

Maybe that smile or that little nod of the head will be the one thing, down the road, that keeps that kid on the right path.

I'll never forget the looks on the faces of all those players when they walked out of the hospitals with me. Every one of them thanked me for giving them the opportunity to touch a few kids who needed a little lift.

Those are the memories that really count. There's a whole lot of new memories out there just waiting to be made. All it takes is a few minutes from all of us.

All we need to do is stoop down to touch a child.

The Universal Manager

No one will ever know if Sparky would have been a successful manager in anything but baseball.

"Why the hell wouldn't he have been?" Pete Rose asked. "He knows people. He cares about them. He can motivate. Isn't that how all good businesses should be run?"

In Sparky's business, good players are the key to making a good manager.

Even the great Willie Shoemaker couldn't make a mule run with the thoroughbreds. Given just a halfway decent horse, though, and he was in the race till the finish.

Sparky was the master at not allowing good teams to lose. And once in a while, somehow he even managed to ride a mule into the September stretch.

Sparky attacks all of life's challenges as though he'll never get the chance again.

"He was the best manager of the time since I've been around the game," said St. Louis Manager Tony LaRussa.

LaRussa, who made his managerial debut with the Chicago White Sox in 1979, has more wins than any active manager. He won a World Series with the Oakland Athletics.

"He was the whole package," LaRussa said. "He knew his players. He knew how to deal with the media. Most importantly, he cared about the fans. People in uniform have a responsibility to the fans. There's nobody who takes that responsibility more seriously than Sparky."

Sparky is an old-liner when it comes to protecting the rights of the fan.

"The game belongs to them," Sparky said, "not to anybody actually in baseball. You just try to cheat the fans and you might as well pack up the bats and balls and tell all the boys to save their gas money. The fans pay all the bills."

Sparky's work ethic and reverence for the position of baseball manager ensured that he ran every game as though October was tomorrow.

"Sparky has a big heart," explained Kirk Gibson. "He made us believe that we were never down till the game was over. It didn't matter if we were down six runs in the first inning or ten games out of first place with a month to go in the season . . . we simply never quit. More people ought to approach life that way."

Surrender is never an option in the world according to Sparky. His method of attack made it particularly dangerous to manage against.

"You know that old saying about managing 'by the book'?" asked Tommy Lasorda. "I don't know what the book is supposed to be. Whatever it is, you could throw it out the window with Sparky.

"He never had any set way of managing. Just when you thought you had him cornered, he pulled out another trick. He was always prepared. He had his team prepared. He knew everything about the team he was managing against. Preparation is a two-step head start."

Sparky already had won back-to-back World Championships with the Cincinnati Reds when Lasorda took over the Los Angeles Dodgers in 1977. LaRussa discovered what Lasorda already knew after Sparky made the switch to the American League with the Detroit Tigers.

"He had the right balance of predictability, aggressiveness, and unpredictability," LaRussa explained. "When he knew he had the best of the situation, he kept his hands off and just let the players go out and play. When he knew he was at a disadvantage, all of a sudden he came up with something more aggressive like stealing third base and running a lot more.

"He was very smart about putting his hand in or keeping it out. That's why you saw him win when he had the best players and also win when he didn't. He became more active when he had to, but he was smart enough to know the difference. That's the sign of a great coach, a military officer, a business manager or any type of leader."

Managers, players and coaches agree that Sparky's approach to managing reflected his very approach to life. He was fearless. He didn't live on the edge. He pushed the edge to another limit.

"You couldn't scare him," Lasorda said. "Don't ever try to scare him because he'll just come at you stronger. Give him a dare and he'll get your name when he's done doing business."

LaRussa learned quickly there was no way to intimidate Sparky. It didn't matter if an opposing team had all the better players. Sparky's team might get beat, but it would not be intimidated.

"He did something that few people are able to do," LaRussa explained. "He put fear in the right perspective.

"He didn't want to lose when he thought he should win. He was fearful of ruining his reputation of losing everything he had earned. That kept him on his toes. He was careful about all the things he had to do to be right. When you're successful, it's easy to get comfortable and lazy. He never allowed that to become the case. When it came to a challenge or a controversy, he was not fearful. He'd confront any player and any competition."

A manager defines the spirit of a team. Players are reflections of that spirit. If a manager tiptoes into a game always reacting to a situation instead of creating one, players generally perform in the same manner. If a manager walks fearlessly and forces the opposition to respond, players build confidence. They know when their leader is in control.

In his role as All-Star catcher for the Tigers, Lance Parrish got a closer look than most at the confidence his manager generated.

"He wasn't afraid to make a decision," Parrish said. "When he made it, he never backed down."

Parrish was particularly impressed with the way his manager handled pitching changes. Sparky never sent his pitching coach out to make a switch. If the Tigers were getting hammered, he accepted the jeering from the crowd almost as a personal challenge.

"He always jumped up out of the dugout and let the people boo and yell whatever they wanted to," Parrish recalled. "When he was ready to leave the mound, he'd smile and tell me to listen to the fans as he walked back to the dugout.

"When he got back, he'd stand there for a split second and let them boo a little more. I think it was his way of letting them know that it was O.K. to boo him, but he wasn't going to change. I got a kick out of that. I never saw him get intimidated by anyone."

Except for only three others, Sparky managed more big league games than anybody in history. Even after 26 years, he embraced the challenge of each single game. It never mattered whether the team needed a win to clinch a title or if the team was ten games out of first place with only nine games to play. No one game was less important than any other.

"When he retired after the 1995 season, I know he could have continued," said Alan Trammell. "There was no one outmanaging him. We were a little short on personnel, but that never stopped him.

"He was always on top of things. He was always thinking a couple of innings ahead. He never got surprised by a move some other manager made. Usually, it was something Sparky had done to force that move."

Managers like LaRussa appreciate Sparky's professionalism.

"He was the classic competitor," LaRussa said. "But in a high level way. He competed in the highest degree and tried to beat you any way he could. But he never embarrassed you. I always admired that quality. He was always willing to share the things he had learned with all of us who wanted to learn from him."

Sparky was unafraid to counsel competing managers. He never viewed them as a threat . . . only as a challenge.

"A lot of young managers were intimidated by his success and stature," LaRussa said. "So he took it upon himself to let us know he was always approachable.

"He always sought out a young manager before a game to see how he was doing. He has very high standards. If someone was insincere with him and didn't measure up—especially in sportsmanship—then you saw Sparky's hard side. He wants everyone to share high standards. If you fall short with something you can control, he's unforgiving."

The old baseball maxim that "a manager is hired to be fired" is almost universally applied to anyone who takes the job. John McGraw was fired. So was the legendary Casey Stengel.

Sparky was fired from Cincinnati. He was nudged out from Detroit. The fact that he managed for only two teams during a 26-year run is testimony to his baseball savvy and his ability to lead men.

"He could have managed a supermarket or an assembly line," Rose said. "He happened to choose baseball. What the hell's the difference?

"Sparky is a leader. He can get a group of guys pointed in one direction. All he cared about was winning. Isn't that what leadership is all about?"

Somehow the fans are glad he chose the Reds and Tigers instead of Freddy's Supermarket in Cincinnati or Detroit.

It's People First

If a man can't handle himself, then he don't have no business trying to manage a team of ball players or a team of horses.

If he's gonna try to manage a team, then he better realize that all those guys in uniform are people first before they're players.

One of the biggest mistakes any young man can make is to believe that he is gonna be the best manager since Casey Stengel just because he knows something about the game.

I don't care if he knows how much chalk goes into making the foul lines. If he don't first know how to deal with people, then he don't know nothing. He could memorize all the record books from cover to cover and still not know how to manage a team any better than the guy selling the Cracker Jack.

Baseball ain't no different than any other kind of job. A good manager is a leader. He ain't afraid to tell one of his people when they make a mistake. He ain't afraid to pat somebody on the back when they deserve it.

And sure as hell, he ain't afraid to lose his job. If you tippy-toe around, always looking over your shoulder waiting for someone to catch you, I'll guarantee you're gonna get caught.

Walk in fear and fear will gobble you up. Fear is always hungry for cowards.

There ain't no big dark secret to managing in the

major leagues. In fact, some of the best managers never make it to the majors at all. Who cares what level you happen to be part of—major leagues or Little Leagues? If you love the game and really are a true leader, then you're gonna help to teach some people. That's all that matters.

The word "leader" means that people are gonna follow you. They look up to you. They depend on you. That means you better know where you're going or everybody is gonna wind up down the road in the middle of a cabbage patch.

It's impossible to lead people if you don't take the time to find out what makes them tick. If one of your people is looking for a pat on the back or just a little smile, you're gonna lose him forever if you kick him in the butt. You've got to find out what he's thinking.

In baseball, I've seen so many managers make the same mistake. They demand that their players understand them. It ain't up to the players to understand the manager. It's up to the manager to understand his team.

You can't make a turtle run like a rabbit. So if you ain't got no rabbits, don't be trying to steal bases with a shell on your back.

People always say that a good manager can win 10 to 15 extra games a year.

I say that's a bunch of baloney.

I ain't never seen a manager yet who has put on a glove or picked up a bat or fired a baseball to win any games. Nobody will ever convince me that a manager wins games. I would like for somebody to show me how that's done.

The difference between a good manager and an average one is simple. The good ones don't lose what their boys already have filed away in the win column. The good ones know how to protect a lead once they get into the eighth and ninth innings. They're defensive managers. Ain't nobody gonna pick their pockets when the game is on the line.

There's gonna be times when something screwy happens and the lead just disappears. Remember what Bernie Carbo and Carlton Fisk did to me in the sixth game of the 1975 World Series?

For the good managers, that don't happen more than five times a year.

Bad things just sort of happen to bad managers. They'll let 15 games a year slip away.

If you've done your homework and prepared yourself and your team the best that you can, there ain't much more to do once that first pitch is thrown.

I remember when Lou Piniella had just taken over as the Yankee manager. When we met at home plate with the umpires, I looked over at Lou and said, "Are you done?"

He wasn't sure what I meant. He said, "I guess I am."

I told him now we can go back to the dugout and enjoy the game. There wasn't a whole lot more for us to do until it got to the eighth or ninth. Then the man with the lead better know how to protect it. I know one thing for sure . . . I was gonna try to pick his pocket clean.

I always had a soft spot for the young manager. He's trying not to show it, but inside those knickers he's wearing, his knees are knocking.

I know. I've been there. A manager can be surrounded by 50,000 people and he's the loneliest person in that park.

Whenever a new young man came into the league, I always made it a point to visit him during batting practice. It wasn't his job to come to me. I was supposed to go see him. I already had been through some wars. That young man was just getting used to the battle.

I really got pumped up when I was going up against one of the real good ones. When I was with Cincinnati, my wife, Carol, didn't even have to look at the schedule. She knew when Montreal came to town. She knew by the way I acted. I always wanted to go up against Gene Mauch.

Gene ain't in the Hall of Fame, but he should be. He managed 26 years in the big leagues. He needed just 8 games more for 4,000. That's Hall of Fame numbers. I don't care what kind of record he had.

Gene was the master. He knew my players just like I knew his. That's the way I always prepared against a team. I tried to figure what kind of moves I'd make if I had the other guys.

Managing a baseball team ain't much different than managing a group of people in almost any other kind of job.

The people are people first. If you treat them like you care, prepare yourself for any kind of situation and then work till you can't work no more, then you've done your job. Something crazy might happen, but it's out of your control.

If you are prepared, you can look in the mirror without second-guessing yourself about anything that could have been.

There's no tricks . . . only preparation. It's the best tool any manager can have.

DID HE SAY THAT?

When he was in high school, Sparky "never got no A" in English.

Even back then, he mixed words like a chef tosses a salad. He jumbled phrases. He sliced sentences with the finesse of a machete.

"A semicolon belongs to a guy who had half his stomach taken out," he cracks when asked about proper punctuation.

His misuse of proper English can turn a teacher's hair whiter than his own. His message, though, generally hits the bull's-eye more squarely than a Sunday morning television preacher.

Often with a whole lot more sense.

"As long as people know what I'm talking about, there ain't no sense worrying about periods and commas and all them other squiggly creatures," Sparky says.

No one is better at breathing life into a dead story than Sparky. As a manager, he was the media's best friend.

He's always good for a story. He makes it difficult for a writer to walk away without feeling good.

For Sparky, the media has never been an adversary. Instead, most writers consider him a friend.

His natural flair for drama makes him a magnet for all media types. For whatever innate reason, he always has a sense for what a writer needs.

During the baseball season, Sparky's bent for entertainment usually dictated the tone of daily coverage. He treated writers from the nation's leading daily newspapers no more deferentially than those from local weeklies. He had a love affair with the cameras and microphones that fawned over every word.

"No person could ever have been more cognizant of what his role with the media involved than Sparky," remarked Tom Gage. "He never wanted any reporter to leave his office disappointed. It was always an adventure and a pleasure to go into his office."

Gage is the veteran baseball writer for *The Detroit News*. He covered Sparky throughout his entire managerial career in Detroit.

Obviously, Sparky's expertise for handling the media is a gift. There's no way to learn it even after a lifetime in the game.

Sparky certainly never had any formal training. For whatever reason, though, he always knows exactly what the media wants.

Sparky is aware of the audience he's reaching. He understands the difference between a straight game story and a feature that requires interpretation.

After giving the morning newspaper one story, he could turn the subject around to the satisfaction of a writer who was more interested in quotes. He felt almost compelled to create a completely fresh perspective.

No one sparkles better on camera. With his trademark white hair and a chiseled face that has been through thousands of baseball wars, few in history were ever more photogenic.

"The only thing he didn't like were for microphones to be pushed into his face," Gage recalled. "Other than that, he'd talk until the writers got tired. He almost seemed obsessed with filling an empty notebook."

Sparky pontificated daily with writers on matters pertaining to baseball history, the current state of the game, and any subject that demands an opinion. Life according to Sparky has always been a favorite subject of the national sporting press.

A sharp writer properly equipped with questions could walk away with enough material to fill a column for the next couple of weeks.

If the writer didn't have the questions, Sparky usually spit out answers anyway.

"Every morning I used to pick up my paper and wonder what the little man got himself into this time," joked Sparky's former boss Jim Campbell. "I used to call him Chief Walking Eagle. He was too full of baloney to fly."

Not only is the nonstop chatter part of his very essence, Sparky truly believes that creating stories through the media is part of the game's romance.

In the 1975 World Series, for instance, Sparky was prepared for the immense, and often caustic, Boston media. Going back to the days of Ted Williams, the Boston media has enjoyed a reputation for being one of the most critical brotherhoods in either league.

Sparky had been warned about veteran *Boston Globe* writer Cliff Keane. Keane had been a fixture on the Boston baseball beat for decades. He had great insight into the game, but also possessed an acidic sense of humor. He dared one of his subjects not to get riled.

When the Series opened in Boston, an army of writers crammed into Sparky's tiny office in the back of Fenway Park's visiting clubhouse. The manager of The Big Red Machine was about to hold court.

"Hey, Busher," Keane greeted Sparky to break the ice of the overcrowded room. "Busher" is a demeaning term universally used in baseball to describe a manager or player who comes from the minor leagues—or the "bushes."

Sparky smiled and quickly jumped out of his chair. He wiggled his way through all the cramped shoulders to stand in front of where Keane was seated. Sparky then bent over and planted a kiss on the top of Keane's balding head.

"I just want you to know . . . that's the way we National Leaguers treat you guys in the American League," Sparky cracked.

The room exploded into laughter. The tone had been set for one of history's great World Series. Whatever might transpire on the field, the national media had been cleverly served notice that the upcoming classic was going to be fun.

Sparky's relationship with the media always has been a

two-way love affair. The media's admiration for the little manager is easily understood. Even under the most dire circumstances, Sparky never fails to perform.

In turn, Sparky loves to play with the media. He was always acutely aware of how to shape his answers for the benefit of his team.

He's a showman. And what better way to remain on center stage than to befriend the people who can keep the spotlight shining?

"Sparky has always taken great pride in being a story," Gage said. "But he's also lived up to the responsibility that goes along with it."

At times, certain segments of the media became very parochial about Sparky. Some representing the larger media outlets felt he belonged exclusively to them.

Sparky's approach was much more innocent. Whoever asked the question first got the first answer. Whoever asked the best one never walked away disappointed.

In 1979, for instance, after it had just been announced in Detroit that he was going to take over the Tigers, the telephones in his Thousand Oaks home rang like an alarm clock factory. At the time, Sparky had two separate lines.

He was speaking to *Detroit Free Press* sports columnist Jim Hawkins on one line when Sparky's wife, Carol, informed him that Howard Cosell was waiting on the other. Cosell was a renowned New York broadcaster who exercised considerable influence on the national sports scene.

"Tell him to call back," Sparky told Carol. "Tell him I'm on the line with the press."

Sparky was considered to be the unofficial Pied Piper of baseball. He also knew how to manipulate the media to the advantage of his team.

When his team was struggling or had dropped a particularly tough game, Sparky had the ability to keep an onslaught of media members in his office just long enough for his players to cool in the clubhouse. Even some of the veterans aware of the tactic were hesitant to leave his room. Sparky threw out just enough bait to lure them into thinking he was about to say something big.

"He was shrewd, but he knew he had to do his job," Gage said. "He's as sharp a street-smart person as you'll ever meet."

Sparky constantly schooled his players on the importance of cooperation with the media.

"He taught us that they had a job to do, too," Pete Rose said. "Sometimes we might not like what they were doing, but it was better to cooperate than to start a war. He always said if they write one bad story and you just ignore it, then the affair is dead. If you try to attack them, then they're just gonna write another story about the attack.

"He knew how to use the press without them knowing he was pulling the strings. Just when they thought they were getting the better of him, he picked their pockets cleaner than bleach."

Lance Parrish was particularly impressed with the way Sparky prepared a young team for dealing professionally with the media.

"A lot of guys had trouble dealing with the media after bad games," Parrish said. "Sparky let us know it wasn't fair to treat the media any differently than we would treat anybody else. They had a job to do. He tried to get us to appreciate the professions of other people.

"He did everybody a big favor. As an athlete, you come to realize the media can be either very helpful or very harmful. A lot of guys come to understand that later in their careers and regret a lot of the things they did before."

Sparky spent considerable time trying to make Kirk Gibson understand his role with the media. No player had to worry how Sparky handled the press.

"As long as you did your job on the field, he protected you in the press," Gibson said. "He called all the shots and never blamed a player if a play failed. He always told us, 'I don't care if you look stupid. I will tell them in the paper that I told you to do it.' And he always did. He never got on a guy in the paper unless some guy asked for it. That's class. Class is what separated Sparky from everybody else."

The single element in all professional sports that has

changed most drastically since when Sparky first started to manage is the unbridled proliferation of the media.

Instead of just a couple of beat writers and the occasional columnist, teams now are blanketed with every type of media exposure. Television, in particular, has invaded sports' most inner sanctums. Television's overwhelming shadow is always present. Its instantaneous coverage has forced newspapers and magazines to dig deeper into the personal lives of the performers they cover.

This ubiquitous media eye has led to certain ugly encounters between some members of the media and those players who resist the change.

Sparky adapted gracefully. In fact, he welcomed the added exposure.

There's never been a notepad that can't use one more Sparkyism. There's never been a camera that's gone begging for one more Sparky picture.

Even for Sparky, the job can be taxing. Really, though, he wouldn't want it any other way.

Honesty and Humor

There are two rules I follow when I deal with the media—always tell the truth and try to have a few laughs along the way.

That ain't a bad way to approach anything in life.

I never knew nothing about newspapers except that's where I could look up all the scores. I always watched television and listened to radio, but I never dreamed anybody would actually want me to appear on them.

I never had no training about what to say or when to bite my tongue. So it's best to keep it simple—honesty and fun.

I really get a laugh out of people who think they can make things better by telling lies. They ain't fooling nobody but themselves.

It might take a little while, but somehow the truth is always gonna creep out. You can lie to the press . . . you can lie to a priest . . . you can lie to your boss . . . you can lie to your wife. Eventually that lie is gonna bite you like a rattlesnake.

Have you ever seen anybody who could tell just one lie? After that first one, they have to cover up with another. Before you know it, they're spitting them out like watermelon seeds. They get so confused they don't know the truth themselves. That's because they can't remember the first lie.

If you tell the truth the first time, you don't have to worry about nothing. My mama used to say it's like a shot of castor oil. The truth might hurt, but it ain't gonna kill you. Once you tell the truth, then it's up to the next guy to deal with it.

There were times during my career when I couldn't say nothing to the press about a player or something going on with the club. That wasn't lying. Once in a while I did use my brain instead of my tongue.

If you tell just one lie, you're a liar for the rest of your life. Why should anyone ever believe a liar? If you tell the truth, who cares what other people think?

If you don't have fun doing what you're doing, then you shouldn't be doing it in the first place.

The office or the factory or the school room ain't a comedy club. But you can get a lot more done wherever you are if you take the time to enjoy yourself.

I might be old-fashioned, but I always believed baseball was supposed to be fun. Part of the fun are all the stories that get collected over the years. Once the games are done, they're dead. The stories live forever. They keep the game alive.

I've always enjoyed playing around with the press. They're looking for a story. I'm trying to make my team look good. So why not work together and have a few laughs along the way?

I never dreamed the press would get as big as it is today. You can't turn around today without bumping into a writer or a cameraman. They're ready to shoot whatever you're doing.

When I first started, we had a couple of regular writers. It was pretty much the same in every city we played. I knew who to expect at every stop. I knew what kind of guys they were and pretty much the way they worked.

Now it's totally different. Sometimes for a big series, there's just as many writers and radio and TV people like there used to be for the Playoffs. That's more pressure on the manager and the players, but it's good for the sport.

What the players must remember is how lucky they are to be there. There's gonna come a day when nobody wants to talk to them. Instead of people asking them for autographs, those same players will be begging to give them away.

Everyone has a job to do. And everyone deserves to be treated with respect.

I always try to remember first names. If you greet people with a smile and call them by their names, you've got them on your side right from the start.

And what's so wrong with being nice? They've got a job to do, too.

That's what I always tried to make my players understand. The media ain't no different than anybody else. If you answer their questions honestly, there ain't nothing left to do.

A manager sometimes has to tap dance with the press. If they're coming from the east, you gotta head west. You gotta circle around the boys and not get yourself trapped.

The manager must be honest. But he better know how to answer those questions better than the press knows how to ask them.

I always enjoyed that part. I liked it when they tried to pin me down on something. It kept me sharp.

There were times when I started the circling myself. I knew when I had to keep the press away from my boys. There were times when my boys needed a few minutes alone. I wanted them to talk with their heads, not their emotions.

I'd start a story that kept everybody in my office. Sometimes it made sense. Other times I wondered myself—what the heck am I talking about?

A good manager has to do that. He must be able to protect his players.

Some managers have trouble with the media. They're not so much afraid of the media as they are of themselves.

I never was afraid of nobody or nothing. I believed in myself and all the people around me. I never let the press or anybody else intimidate the way I think.

The media can't hurt you if you don't let it. In my 26 years of managing, I bet the media helped me 95% of the time. That 5% they got me was a pretty fair trade-off.

I never looked at the media as the enemy. And I never judged a writer by the size of his paper. If someone asked the right question, he got the right answer. Some of the better writers actually came from the smaller papers.

A young man from a radio school came to interview me when I managed in Cincinnati. He was so scared, he almost dropped his tape recorder when he shook my hand.

I walked around my desk and told him, "Young man, this is gonna be easy. You write down three questions. When I get to the end of one, I'll tap you on the knee and then you pick up with the next one."

We got through the interview and his face lit up like a Christmas tree. I told him, "That wasn't so tough. Don't you ever be nervous when you're prepared."

It all gets down to being nice to people. What does it cost you to be nice to somebody who's just trying to do his job?

It don't cost a dime. And in the long run, you're gonna end up richer for it.

A Bogey and a Smile

The ten-minute drive from Sparky's house to the Sunset Hills Country Club takes only five minutes with Sparky behind the wheel.

He's not reckless. The drive has just become so routine that it's simple to slip down Olsen Road and wind through the hills that hug the course which Sparky has made home.

As he zips down Mountclef Road out of the subdivision, he shouts hello and shoots one-liners at neighbors. They wave and smile at their animated friend.

To them, he's simply George Anderson. A very good neighbor. He and his wife, Carol, have lived in the same house since the day the neighborhood was built 30 years ago. At least by sight, Sparky knows everybody.

When he pulls into Sunset Hills' parking lot, he aims his car at the first open space. There may be one closer to the clubhouse, but he's anxious to play. He can dash up there quicker than the car can maneuver another row.

Once on the first tee, Sparky feels relaxed.

"Carol had to shoot him four cups of coffee before he left the house, but this is the time he feels the best," said Billy Consolo who has been a friend for more than 50 years.

Most of the time, the match is the same. There's Jack Luinstra, a retired commercial airline pilot. He's lived across the street from Sparky for more than 30 years. There's Pete Daley, a retired salesman who also spent seven years in the big leagues as a backup catcher. Then there's Consolo, former major league utility infielder who coached with Sparky throughout his Tiger career.

Sparky is the catalyst. He sets the tee time. He calls his

"boys" to make sure they're on time. He's been jabbering from the time he parked the car. Now it's time to toss tees for teams. The match is big—a dollar a man.

One dollar or a million, the money doesn't matter. For Sparky and his boys, only the competition counts.

Sparky feels safe here. Except for visiting the grandkids, nothing makes him more content.

Sunset Hills is picturesque without pretense. It lacks the prestige of nearby clubs like Riviera, Bel-Air, Sherwood and the Los Angeles Country Club.

He's played all of them. In fact, he's been offered memberships.

He simply prefers Sunset Hills. He feels suffocated by anything hinting of pretense.

Sunset Hills is cozy and comfortable. More important to Sparky, it's a club where he knows almost everyone by their first names. And everyone there knows him as plain old "George."

Sparky's golf game is best described as "legalized mayhem." He never sneaks up on a course. He attacks it with a kamikaze charge that starts the moment he pulls into the parking lot.

Finesse has never been part of Sparky's golf game. Some describe it more like a jackhammer stirring a milk shake.

"We're always trying to get him to cut down on his swing," Consolo chuckled. "I was standing on the tee one time when the head of his club broke off and hit me in the chest. He swung so hard he broke the club.

"I was standing behind him. I told him there's no safe place to stand when he's hitting. The safest place is probably in the middle of the fairway."

Whether or not a club is broken, it rarely stays in his bag for too long.

"He bought the Alien for $125," Consolo said. "He saw it advertised on TV. First time he used it, he smoked one right down the middle and said it was the greatest club he ever hit.

"Someone else has it now. When he hits too many bad shots with a club, he gives it away. His bag is a collection of mongrels. Everybody in Thousand Oaks must have one of his old clubs."

It doesn't matter to Sparky. He simply enjoys being on the course with his friends.

"Half the time he doesn't know what he's doing," Daley said shaking his head. "Before two holes are finished, though, he's telling everybody else how to play.

"I bet he's quit the game a thousand times. But he always comes back. He loves it and he's so much fun to be around. He's just one of the boys."

Sparky still has to spend some time away from home. He delivers speeches around the country. He is particularly adept at filming television commercials. He also serves as a color commentator for home Anaheim Angels telecasts.

The rest of his time is split between visiting his grandkids and playing 90-something golf with the boys with regular names like Jack and Pete and Billy.

One reason for his expanded time on the golf course was the sudden and unspectacular halt to his managerial career.

Among some of his closer friends, there is strong speculation that Sparky has been unofficially "blackballed" from baseball because he refused to manage replacement players during the strike-plagued spring training of 1995.

When that season finished, Sparky was only sixty-one years old. He remains perfectly healthy.

Since that time there have been a number of managerial changes. In spite of winning more games in history than only two other managers . . . in spite of bringing any club a walking-talking, full-service public relations package . . . Sparky has not received a serious offer to manage.

"I do not believe I've been blackballed," he says. "Baseball has been too good to me and too many other people for me to believe anything like that could happen."

Nevertheless, the absence of baseball's most celebrated ambassador of goodwill remains a curious omission. Especially in a sport with myriad public relations problems and still struggling for fan support after the devastating cancellation of the 1994 World Series.

Sparky doesn't waste a minute even thinking about the

speculation. He thoroughly enjoys making up for lost time with his family and playing golf with the kind of guys people bump into every day.

In a couple of summers Sparky and all of his fans will convene in Cooperstown, New York for the biggest celebration of his career.

Sparky becomes eligible for induction into Baseball's Hall of Fame in the year 2000. His peers, the media and fans all over the country, already have proclaimed Sparky to be a Hall of Famer just waiting to happen.

"He's a Hall of Fame person, not just a Hall of Fame manager," said Joe Morgan, who already has been enshrined. "Can you even imagine the Hall of Fame without Sparky in it? He's done more for baseball than night games. He means even more than that to all the people he's touched."

Requirements for membership stretch far beyond all the records and statistics that make up the guts of the game. Membership in this brotherhood requires more than excellence on the field. It demands moral character. Members must honorably represent the game that has symbolized American sportsmanship for almost a century.

Until the time comes, Sparky is quite content playing golf, playing with his grandkids, and playing the same person he's remained his entire life.

"I don't know why it is, but he really treasures being around average people," said Charles Fieweger who also lives in Thousand Oaks and has known Sparky for 20 years.

"Maybe it's because he's had so much of the other stuff. He can't go anywhere without being recognized. But he doesn't need it. His greatest asset is his loyalty. He's loyal to God, his family, his friends, and the city he lives in. And about in that order."

Daley had a front row seat watching another American sports legend cope with stardom. He spent part of his big league career as a teammate of Ted Williams. He remembers how Williams was hounded by the press and the public wherever he traveled.

Because of the explosion in media coverage and America's

near religious fanaticism about celebrity, demands on Sparky's personal time have intensified since the height of Williams' notoriety.

"He's very stable from the standpoint of realism and honesty," Daley said. "What you see is what you get. There's nothing phony about Sparky. He's always polite to people even though there are times when it inconveniences him."

So that five-minute cruise from the foot of Sparky's driveway to the first available space in the Sunset Hills lot will continue to be traveled.

The routine has about as much chance for change as Sparky switching his approach to the way he treats people.

The chance for that is about the same as for him breaking par—absolutely none at all.

And Still Not a Dime

First of all, I ain't been blackballed.

People are free to think whatever they want. All I know is I spent 43 years in the greatest game God ever gave us. If that ain't enough to be grateful for, then somebody better tell me what I missed.

Even if it was true, what difference does it make? I couldn't change it anyway so what's the sense in worrying?

Nobody had it better than me for 26 years in the major leagues. If that ain't being treated right by baseball, then I'd like to see how somebody is treated wrong.

Baseball is a whole lot bigger than Sparky Anderson. Does anybody really think that something so great is going to change everything they do over one person like me?

That really makes no sense.

The game is bigger than all of us. I never knocked it when I made my decision and I ain't about to knock it now. It's been too good to me . . . too good to my family . . . and too good to every kid in America who ever put on a glove.

Besides, I'm happy. I play golf and play with my grandkids. Now which one of those am I supposed to give up?

I've got no regrets. None for what I did and none for what I didn't do.

I do believe baseball has problems, though. I think all our sports do.

I don't sit around thinking how great it was in the "good old days." Whether those days were really all that good or they just seem to get better the longer they're gone doesn't matter.

The bottom line is they're gone. We can stand on one leg blindfolded and whistle "Dixie" and they still ain't coming back. So let's move on. But we better learn from our mistakes. We better make things better right now.

Sports are just like everything else in our lives. Times have changed.

Look at politics. We've reached the point where we wouldn't trust our cousin if he was in office. Look at our families. It's really scary how many families have the father and mother working and the kids are left to grow up by themselves. They teach things in school now that none of us ever dreamed about.

So naturally sports had to change.

Not everything that used to be was better than it is now. But anybody who thinks that sports don't have a pack of problems ain't watching the same games I've loved ever since I was a kid.

I think the biggest problem we gotta address right now is who the games belong to.

They don't belong to the owners with all their power and all the money that they made from all their other businesses. They don't belong to the players who make a million dollars a month. Some of those guys walk around like they're doing the fans a favor just by showing up to the park.

The games belong to the fans. Fans are the real owners. They wind up paying all the bills. They also could pull the plug if they ever get fed up enough with some of the nonsense that is going on.

One of the saddest days in my life occurred on January 6th, 1997. That was the day I heard that the O'Malley family was putting the Los Angeles Dodgers up for sale.

Can anyone imagine anybody but the O'Malley family owning the Dodgers?

I don't blame the O'Malleys one bit. But with them gone, there ain't none of the baseball families around that made the game what it is.

The game has gone corporate. The gray suits are here for good now because none of the families are left. The game ain't never gonna be the way it was.

But let's don't forget what baseball really means. It's about kids playing the game. It's about rooting for the home team. It's about kids learning how to win and lose honestly in life on a playing field. It's about mom and pop having enough money to take the kids to the park. It's about clubs and players alike caring for the fans as much as the fans care about them.

Kids learn more about the important things in life from sports than they do from any schoolbook. Sports teach kids honesty. They teach respect. They teach discipline.

There's no black and white or any other colors in sports. Victories go to the teams that work the hardest and prepare the best. Even the losers learn from sports. Life ain't easy. How a kid learns to handle defeat goes a long way toward how he manages the rest of his life.

We made a big mistake in baseball. All the marketing hype in the world can't fix a love affair that never shouldda been broken in the first place.

I get a real kick out of watching some of the gimmicks that the marketeers use. They try to bring back old-time feelings about the way the game used to be. They're trying to re-create a feeling that they helped to snuff out!

How in the heck do you market a love affair? You can't manufacture love. Either it's there or it ain't! You don't need a fancy degree in marketing or law to figure that out.

Why do football and basketball seem to draw all the attention? Let's form a committee of owners and players and veterans to find out what went wrong. And once we find out the answers, let's be big enough people to admit our mistakes. Let's try to come up with some solutions to put the game back on track.

Why ain't more kids playing baseball on the sandlots? Why ain't they playing stickball in the streets?

They used to. There has to be a reason for this failure. Failure is not just an accident.

I don't care what you do in life. If you can stand up and say you failed, then you have honor. And if you have honor and really want to make things right, then you can fix almost any problem.

I don't have all the answers, but I know where I would start. For two weekends of every month during the season, I'd let all kids under fourteen years old into every park for free. And I'd do it for the next 10 years. We have got to bring a new generation of fans into our game. If we mean it, we've got to show them that we really care about them. Maybe then they would pass this same feeling on to their kids.

The owners might laugh at this, but we've got to get kids thinking more about baseball. This game is too precious not to share it with our kids.

The marketing thing has become a madness. I hear talk on TV about one club having "out-merchandised" all the other teams.

Now isn't that something to be proud of?

All the mothers and fathers work pretty hard to make a living. They want to give their kids a little extra. And now one team should be praised for coming up with more ways to sell their merchandise than the other teams?

Today there are teams with three different kinds of

hats. What about the kids who want all three? That's $60 that mom and pop have to shell out.

There are tee-shirts and jackets and sweat bands and who knows what else.

Marketing is fine. It's part of our lives. But when we start changing logos and uniforms every couple of years just to sell something new, I think we're going to mom and pop with our hands out a little too often. They have a right to be turned off.

Maybe I'm old-fashioned. But I believe if you milk the public too much, eventually they're gonna quit coming up with the milk. People get tired of the old milk job. And when they get tired enough, they don't want to see you around no more.

Maybe we ought to find new ways to get kids interested in playing baseball. If you get them playing when they're young, I guarantee you'll see them at the park when they have families of their own.

What if every club sponsored two teams in each major city? The teams would have to supply all the equipment and all the instruction. A scout in the area would supervise the operation.

Don't you think in 10 to 20 years we might return strong baseball back into the inner-city? And think about the help we could give the mothers and fathers who worry that their kids get into trouble because they don't have nothing to do.

The players have to learn that they're part of the solution, too.

Guys today jump from one team to another for $20 to $30 million. My stomach turns when they say "money really wasn't a factor."

Sure it wasn't . . . as long as there was enough of it.

They say they've always wanted to play in a certain city. Sure, they do. As long as there are two Brinks trucks waiting outside with all the cash.

I've always believed that if you find good fortune in a

city, you have a responsibility to give something back to that community.

Why not give it back by trying to help some youngsters learn how to play the game? All they want is a chance of their own.

I've been very fortunate. I can take care of my family. I can go out every day and play golf with my friends. But I never forget how good baseball has been to all of us. We owe it to the game and all the fans to make it the best sport in America.

Talking about the "good old days" ain't gonna make nothing better. But owners and players worrying about nothing except how to make an extra dollar ain't gonna do nothing but make things worse.

We've got to solve these problems together. We've got to give all the kids a chance to love this game the same way we got that chance.

Maybe it ain't the game that changed. Maybe it's just the people.

Now that I've had some time, I've heard the talk about me maybe going into the Hall of Fame.

When I think about it, though, my goosebumps get goosebumps.

The Hall of Fame ain't just about getting elected. It's not for today. It's not for tomorrow. It's for eternity.

As long as the world exists, the Hall of Fame will be there. That leaves something for your children . . . their children . . . their children's children . . . and all along down the line.

That's what means so much to me. When someone makes it, his grandkids can say, "that's my grandpa." And their kids can say, "that's my great grandpa."

Nobody can ever take that away. Nobody can buy it. Not even Bill Gates and all his zillions.

I know all my records. I'm proud of them and ain't ashamed to talk about them.

But the Hall of Fame is a lot more than numbers. If

you make it into the Hall of Fame, you've done something for baseball a lot more important than all the numbers in the world.

You did your profession proud. You represented it with class. You gave a little something back instead of just filling your pockets along the way.

Whatever anyone does in life, no one makes it to the top alone. You don't make it nowhere without your family, your friends and all the people who cared enough about you to show you the right way.

There's an old saying—"Sports doesn't build character . . . it reveals it."

Nobody makes it to the Hall of Fame without character.

You don't have to be in the Hall of Fame to be a Hall of Fame type person. You don't even need to be in baseball.

A person with class knows how to treat people right. What difference does it make what a person does for a living? Sometimes the guy flipping pancakes has more class than the guy who owns the restaurant. I'll take the guy with class even if he's a bad flipper.

Walter Alston is a manager who made it to the Hall of Fame. I learned one of the greatest lessons of my life when I was invited to a farewell luncheon for him.

Walter never liked for anyone to fuss over him. He never liked no fancy parties. This one was at the Biltmore Hotel in Los Angeles. When he showed up, he came in through the back door.

I was sitting next to Danny Ozark and will never forget what he said when Walter walked into the room. Danny coached for Walter for a long time.

"There's a man from Dartown, Ohio," he said. "When he goes back to Dartown, he'll be the same man who came here all those years ago. He never changed."

I believe that's the highest compliment anyone can receive. After all the years and all the wins and all the

World Series and even the Hall of Fame, Walter never changed.

My greatest hope, now that I'm gone, is that people think the same about me. I hope they say that he came, he never stole, and he also gave something back along the way.

I never hurt nobody. I never cheated. I never tried to climb over someone's back.

I tried to treat people the way I want to be treated. That's what my daddy taught me. That's the way I did it.

And it didn't cost me a dime.

And in Closing

The 1987 Tigers unexpectedly found themselves in one of the wildest pennant races of modern history.

It was exciting for the entire state. Nothing stirs community pride like an old-fashioned baseball pennant race. Suddenly everybody's a fan.

For the manager, players, and organization though, the madness almost makes the games seem incidental. Modern media demands sometimes make finding time to play a game a struggle itself.

Sparky, of course, has always been a media darling. He can't say no to a camera or a microphone. It's during such times the character lives on center stage.

That also happened to be the summer Sparky picked to create his charity for underprivileged kids. Founding a charity at any time is like cutting down a forest with a single ax. In the heat of a pennant race, it's more like trying to juggle crystal on a freeway in the middle of rush hour.

"Are you crazy," I remember asking Sparky as he scurried his way between preparing his team and shotgun interviews and who knows how many meetings at the hospitals.

"It's for the kids," he said. "There ain't nothing more important. They can't do it by themselves."

For more than 20 years now, I've been blessed by so many images of Sparky. All are precious. But none remain as vivid as his drive to make that charity more than a dream.

Except for God and his family, nothing is more important to Sparky than doing the right thing for children. And that includes baseball.

Even after 20 years, I'm amazed at the real person who makes the Sparky character work.

He's aware of his stature. He simply refuses to act like the national celebrity he is. He's a hamburger and fries sort of guy in a steak and lobster world.

And he's proud of it.

Sparky is a potpourri of several slices of American legend. With a chunk of John McGraw's baseball insight . . . Vince Lombardi's intensity . . . Billy Graham's inspirational persuasion . . . Will Rogers' bent for spinning a story . . . Richard Simmons' energy for not knowing how to sit still . . . Casey Stengel's flair for showmanship . . . Willie Nelson's grandfatherly concern . . . and priceless physical features straight from the drawing board of a Disney cartoonist, Sparky transcends sports as a bona fide sliver of real life Americana.

Yet when you meet him, he's everybody's Uncle Charlie. Even upon first meeting, he treats people as if they had been friends since his days back on the sandlots.

There are no secret pockets or hidden cards up his sleeve. What you see with Sparky is precisely what you get.

Sparky's biggest fault is his inability to say "no." Even when he's tired, he signs every autograph with a smile and thank you. Even when there's no more to say, he fills a couple more pages of every reporter's notebook.

Being nice to people "don't cost a dime," he's preached his whole life. Never has he failed to practice what he preaches.

Sparky doesn't walk into a room. He sort of bounces. He's got more energy than a bee in a bottle. He fractures the English language with the finesse of a jackhammer.

But his words and smile make him everybody's friend.

Honesty and courage are Sparky's strongest qualities. I've never met anyone armed with more of both.

Sparky's refusal to manage replacement players in 1995 was the most courageous decision I've witnessed in 30 years around the game.

He knew the stakes were high. He also knew the right thing to do. Even with those stakes stacked against him, he had the courage not to break.

For too many years now, baseball's image has struggled. While it's been immeasurably successful in creating the multimillion dollar player, it's been woefully remiss in producing the colorful characters that give life to the game.

Sparky truly is one of those characters. But his measure as a man away from the park forever will outshine his heroics on the field.

When Sparky is inducted into the Hall of Fame, all of those wonderful baseball numbers will sparkle for eternity on his plaque.

I'll marvel at their immensity. I'll acknowledge with tender respect their significance to the game.

Then I'll give a wink of thanks for the privilege of knowing Sparky . . . more for the man than one of the game's greatest managers.

Dan Ewald

All I ask of all you young people is that
you never make money your one goal in life.
Make people your life.
And I promise you what a wonderful life it will be.
Love life . . . and it will love you.

SPARKY ANDERSON